Contents

After obtaining an M.A. degree in South and South-East Asian Civilisation (Thai language/art history) at the University of California at Berkeley, Joe Cummings returned to Thailand to research this guide. Fluent in Thai, he has travelled well over 8000 km within the kingdom, by bus, air, train, and sea.

Joe has been studying South-East Asia for the past ten years; he was a Peace Corps volunteer in Thailand, has worked as a translator/interpreter of Thai, and is now working with South-East Asian refugees in the San Francisco area. He has also travelled in Hong Kong, India, Nepal, western Europe, Canada and Mexico.

Acknowledgements
Immeasurable thanks go to my friend and mentor, Bill Kuo. Gratitude also to Steve McCafferty, Thanasuk Sudhides, Achaan Buddhadasa, Don & Siriwan Campbell, All Jassby, and the Tourist Authority of Thailand, for their aid and inspiration.

And a Request
Travel guides are only kept up to date by travelling. If you find errors or omissions in this book we'd very much like to hear about them. As usual the best letters will score a free copy of the next edition or any other Lonely Planet guide if you prefer.

Introduction

Thailand, or Siam as it was called until the 1940s, has never been colonialized by a foreign power, while all of its South-East Asian neighbours have undergone European colonialization (or more recently, ideological domination by Communism — which originated in Europe) at one time or another. True, it has suffered periodic invasions on the part of the Burmese and the Khmers, and was briefly occupied by the Japanese in WW II, but the kingdom was never externally controlled long enough to dampen the Thais' serious individualism. I say serious because the Thais are so often depicted as fun-loving, happy-go lucky folk (which they often are), but this quality is something they have worked to achieve.

This is not to say that Thailand has not experienced any Western influence. Like other Asian countries it has both suffered and benefited from contact with foreign cultures. But the ever-changing spirit of Thai culture has remained dominant, even in modern city life. The end result is that Thailand has much to interest the traveller, historic culture, lively arts, exotic islands, nightlife, a tradition of friendliness and hospitality to strangers, and one of the world's most exciting cuisines.

Travel in this tropical country is fairly comfortable and down-to-earth. The rail, bus, and air travel network is extensive and every place worth visiting is easily accessible. There are many places worth visiting, many sights to see, a multi-faceted culture to experience, and it is all quite affordable by today's international travel standards.

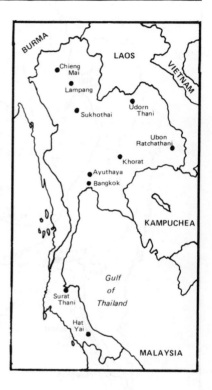

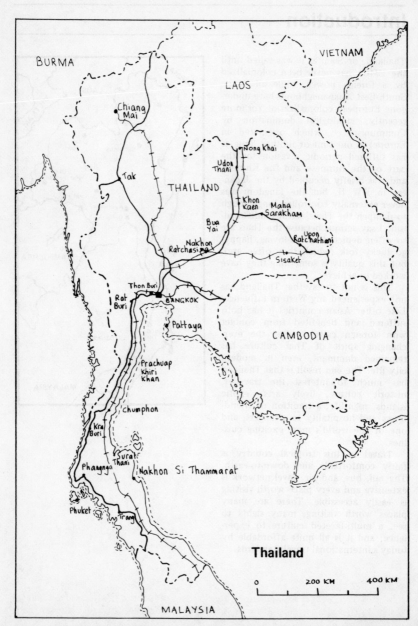

Thailand

BURMA

VIETNAM

LAOS

THAILAND

Chiang Mai

Tak

Nong Khai

Udon Thani

Khon Kaen

Maha Sarakham

Bua Yai

Nakhon Ratchasima

Ubon Ratchathani

Sisaket

Thon Buri

BANGKOK

Rat Buri

Pattaya

CAMBODIA

Prachuap Khiri Khan

Chumphon

Kra Buri

Surat Thani

Phangnga

Nakhon Si Thammarat

Phuket

Trang

MALAYSIA

0   200 KM   400 KM

6

Facts about the Country

GEOGRAPHY

Thailand has an area of 517,000 square km, making it slightly smaller than the state of Texas in the USA or about the size of France. Its longest north to south distance is about 1860 km but its shape makes distances in any other direction quite less. Its shape on the map has been compared to the head of an elephant whose trunk extends down the Malay peninsula, but it looks to me as if someone had squeezed the lower part of the 'boot' of Italy, forcing the volume into the top portion while reducing the bottom. The centre of Thailand, Bangkok, is at about 14° north latitude, putting it on a level with Madras, Manila, Guatemala, and Khartoum. The topography varies and can be divided into four main regions: 1 — the fertile central region, dominated by the Chao Phraya river network; 2 — the north-east plateau, rising some 300 metres above the central plain and the kingdom's poorest region (thanks to 'thin' soil plus occasional droughts/floods); 3 — northern Thailand, a region of mountains and fertile valleys; 4 — the southern peninsular region, which extends to the Malaysian frontier and is predominantly rain forests. The southern region receives the most annual rainfall and the north-east the least, although the north has less general humidity. Thailand's climate is ruled by monsoons, resulting in three seasons; rainy (June-October), cool and dry (November-February), and hot (March-May). More on climate in *Facts for the Visitor).*

PEOPLE

The population of Thailand is 44 million and currently growing at a rate of 1.9% per annum, (as opposed to 3.3% a decade ago and 2.5% in '77) thanks to Khun Mechai's nation-wide family planning campaign. This does not include the recent influx of Lao, Kampuchean, and Vietnamese refugees. About 75% of the citizenry are ethnic Thais, 14% are Chinese, and the remaining 11% include Malayas, the Yumbri, Semang, Moken ('sea gypsies'), Lawa, Kui, Karen, Meo, Yao, Akha, Lahu, Lisu tribes (the latter six are the true hill tribes), Khmers, and Mons. A small number of Europeans and other non-Asians live in Bangkok and Chieng Mai. The literacy rate of Thailand is well above 80% and increasing, and the average life expactancy is 61 years; in both respects Thailand is a leader in the area.

Bangkok is by far the largest city in the kingdom with a population of 4.5 million — too many for the scope of its public services and what little 'city planning' exists. Chieng Mai is second but far behind in population — just over 100,000. All other towns in Thailand have well below 100,000 with few over 20,000.

HISTORY & POLITICS

The history of the geographical area now known as Thailand reaches far back into 'hoary antiquity' as they say. World renowned scholar Paul

Benedict (author of *Austro-Thai Language & Culture*) found that modern linguistic theory, which ties numerous key items in ancient Chinese culture to an early Thai linguistic group, taken together with recent archaeological finds in Thailand, enable us to establish South-East Asia 'as a focal area in the emergent cultural development of homo sapiens. It now seems likely that the first true agriculturists anywhere, perhaps also the first true metal-workers, were Austro-Thai speakers.' These proto-Thais seem to have pro-liferated all over South-East Asia, including the islands of Indonesia, and some may have settled in south and south-west China, later to 're-migrate' to northern Thailand to establish the first Thai kingdom in the 13th century.

With no written records or chronologies it is difficult to say with certain-ty what kind of cultures existed in Thailand before the Christian era. How-ever, by the 6th century AD an important network of agricultural commun-ities was thriving as far south as modern-day Pattani and Yala, and as far north and north-east as Lamphun and Muang Fa Daed (near Khon Kaen). Theravada Buddhism was flourishing and may have entered the region during India's Ashokan period, in the 2nd or 3rd centuries BC, when Indian missionaries were said to have been sent to a land called Suvarnabhumi — 'Land of Gold'. Suvarnabhumi most likely corresponds to a remarkably fertile area stretching from southern Burma, across central Thailand, to eastern Cambodia. Two different cities in the central river basin have long been called Suphanburi, 'City of Gold', and U Thong, 'Cradle of Gold'.

This loose collection of city-states was given the Sanskritic name Dvara-vati, or 'place having gates', the city of Krishna in the Indian epic *Mahabhar-ata*. The French art historian George Coedes discovered the name on some coins excavated in the Nakhorn Pathom area, which seems to have been the centre of Dvaravati culture. The Dvaravati period lasted until the 11th or 12th centuries AD and produced many fine works of art, including distin-ctive Buddha images (showing Indian Gupta influence), stucco reliefs on temples and in caves, some architecture (little of which remains intact), some exquisite terra cotta heads, votive tablets, and other miscellaneous sculpture. Dvaravati may have been a cultural relay point for the pre-Angkor cultures of ancient Cambodia and Champa to the east. The Chinese, through the travels of the famous pilgrim Xuan Zang, knew the area as T'o-lo-po-ti, located between Sriksetra (North Burma) and Tsanapura (Sambor Prei Kuk-Kambuja). The ethnology of the Dvaravati peoples is a controversial subject, though the standard decree is that they were Mons or Mon-Khmers. The Mons themselves seem to have been descended from a group of Indian immigrants from Kalinga, an area overlapping the bound-aries of the modern Indian states of Orissa and Andhra Pradesh. The Dvaravati Mons may have been an ethnic mix of these people and people indigenous to the region, ie the original Thais. In any event, the Dvaravati culture quickly declined in the 11th century under the political domination of the invading Khmers who headquartered themselves in Lopburi. The area around Lamphun, then called Haripunchai, held out until the late 12th century or later as evidenced by the Dvaravati architecture of Wat Kukut in Lamphun.

The Khmer conquest brought Khmer cultural influence in the form of art, language, and religion. Some of the Sanskrit terms in Mon-Thai vocabulary entered the language during the Khmer or Lopburi period, between the 11th and 13th centuries. Monuments from this period, located in Lopburi and Phimai, were constructed in the Khmer style and compare favourably with architecture in Angkor. Elements of Brahmanism, Theravada Buddhism, and Mahayana Buddhism intermixed as Lopburi became a religious centre, and some of each remain to this day in Thai religious and court ceremonies.

While all this was taking place, a distinctly Thai state called Nan Chao (650-1250 AD) was flourishing in what later became Yunnan and Szechuan in China. Nan Chao maintained close relations with imperial China and the two neighbours enjoyed much cultural exchange. The Mongols, under Kublai Khan, conquered Nan Chao in 1253, but long before they came the Thai peoples began migrating southward, homesteading in and around what is today Laos and northern Thailand. They 'infiltrated' South-East Asia in small groups, assimilating the peoples they encountered. Some Thais became mercenaries for the Khmer armies, as depicted on the walls of Angkor Wat, in the early 12th century. The Thais were called 'Syams' by the Khmers, from the Sanskrit *syam* meaning 'dark', in reference to their relatively darker skin colour, and this is how the Thai kingdom eventually came to be called Syam or Siam.

Southern Thailand, the upper Malay peninsula, was under the control of the Srivijaya empire, headquartered in Sumatra, between the 8th and 13th centuries. The regional centre for Srivijaya was Chaiya, near the modern town of Surat Thani, and Srivijaya art remains can still be seen in Chaiya and its environs.

Several Thai principalities in the Mekong valley united in the 13th and 14th centuries and Thai princes took Haripunchai from the Mons to form Lan Na and the Sukhothai region from the Khmers whose Angkor government was declining fast. The Sukhothai kingdom declared its independence in 1238 and quickly expanded its sphere of influence, taking advantage not only of the declining Khmer power but the weakening Srivijaya domain in the south. Sukhothai is considered by the Siamese to be the first true Thai kingdom, and it lasted until annexed by Ayuthaya in 1376 by which time a national identity of sorts had been forged. The second Sukhothai king, Ram Khamheng, organised a writing system which became the basis for modern Thai, and codified the Thai form of Theravada Buddhism, as borrowed from the Sinhalese. Many Thais today view the Sukhothai period with sentimental vision, seeing it as a golden age of Thai politics, religion, and culture — an egalitarian, noble period when everyone had enough to eat and the kingdom was unconquerable. Under Ram Khamheng, Sukhothai extended as far as Nakhorn Si Thammarat in the south, to Vientiane and

Luang Prabang in Laos, and to Pegu in southern Burma. For a short time (1448-1486) the Sukhothai capital was moved to Phitsanuloke.

The Thai kings of Ayuthaya became very powerful in the 14th and 15th centuries, taking over U Thong and Lopburi, former Khmer strongholds, and moving east in their conquests until Angkor was defeated in 1431. Even though the Khmers were their adversaries in battle, the Ayuthaya kings incorporated Khmer court customs and language, with one result being that the Thai monarch gained more absolute authority during the Ayuthaya period and assumed the title *devaraja* — 'god-king', as opposed to the then-traditional *dhammaraja* — 'dharma-king'. In the early 16th century Ayuthaya was receiving European visitors and a Portuguese embassy was established in 1511. The Portuguese were followed by the Dutch (1605), the English (1612), the Danes (1621), and the French (1662).

In the mid-16th century Ayuthaya, and the independent kingdom in Chieng Mai as well, came under the control of the Burmese, but the Thais regained rule of both by the end of the century. Ayuthaya was one of the greatest and wealthiest cities in Asia, a thriving seaport envied not only by the Burmese but by the Europeans who, by their early accounts, were in great awe of the city. It has been said that London, at the time, was a mere village by comparison.

A rather peculiar episode unfolded in Ayuthaya when a Greek, Constantine Phaulkon, became a very high official in Siam under King Narai from 1675 to 1688. He kept out the Dutch and the English but allowed the French to station 600 soldiers in the kingdom. The Thais, fearing a takeover, forcefully expelled the French and executed Phaulkon. Ironically, the word for a 'foreigner' (of European descent) in modern Thai is *farang*, an abbreviated form of *farangset*, meaning 'French'. Siam sealed itself from the west for 150 years following this experience with 'farangs'.

The Burmese again invaded Ayuthaya in 1765 and the capital fell after two years of fierce battle. This time the Burmese really did a job on the city, destroying everything sacred to the Thais, including manuscripts, temples, and religious sculpture. The Burmese, despite their effectiveness in sacking Ayuthaya, could not maintain a foothold in the kingdom, however, and Phya Taksin, a Thai general, made himself king in 1769, ruling from the new capital of Thonburi on the banks of the Chao Phraya river opposite Bangkok. The Thais regained control of their country and further united the disparate provinces to the north with central Siam. Taksin eventually came to regard himself as the next Buddha; his ministers did not approve of this religious fanaticism and he was deposed and executed.

Another general came to power, Chao Phya Chakri, and he was crowned in 1782 under the title Rama I. Rama I moved the royal capital across the river to Bangkok and ruled as the first king of the Chakri dynasty — the present king of Thailand is Rama IX and it has been prophesied that this dynasty will only have nine kings. In 1809 Rama II, son of Rama I, took the throne and reigned through to 1824. Both monarchs assumed the task of restoring the culture so severely damaged by the Burmese decades earlier. Rama III, or Phra Nang Klao (1824-1851), went beyond reviving tradition and developed trade with China while increasing domestic agricultural production.

Rama IV, commonly known as King Mongkut (to the Thais as Phra Chom Klao), was one of the more colourful and innovative of the early Chakri kings. He originally missed out on the throne in deference to his half-brother Rama III and lived as a Buddhist monk for 27 years. During his long monastic term he became adept in the Sanskrit, Pali, Latin, and English languages, studied western sciences, and adopted the strict discipline of local Mon monks. He kept an eye on the outside world and when he took the throne in 1851 he immediately courted diplomatic relations with European nations, while avoiding colonialisation. In addition he attempted to align Buddhist cosmology with modern science to the end of demythologising the Thai religion (a process yet to be fully accomplished), and founded the Thammayut monastic sect, based on the strict discipline he had followed as a monk. The Thammayut remains a minority sect in relation to the Mahanikai who comprise the largest number of Buddhist monks in Thailand. Thai trade restrictions were loosened by King Mongkut and many western powers signed trade agreements with the monarch. He established Siam's first printing press as well, and instituted educational reforms, developing a school system along European lines.

His son, King Chulalongkorn (Rama V, 1868-1910), continued Mongkut's tradition of reform, especially in the legal and administrative realm. Thailand further benefitted from relations with European nations and the USA. Railways were designed and constructed, a civil service established, the legal code restructured. Though Siam still managed to avoid colonialisation, it lost some territory to French Laos and British Burma around this time. King Vajiravudh (Rama VI, 1910-25), during his rather short reign introduced compulsory education and other educational reforms, and further 'westernised' the nation by making the Thai calendar conform to western models.

While Vajiravudh's son King Prajadhipok (Rama VII, 1925-35) ruled, a group of Thai students living in Paris became so enamoured with democratic ideology that they mounted a successful coup d'etat against absolute monarchy in Siam. This bloodless revolution led to the development of a constitutional monarchy along British lines, with a mixed military-civilian group in power. Phibul Songkhram, a key military leader in the 1932 coup, maintained an effective position of power from 1938 until the end of WW II. Rama VIII (Ananda Mahidol), a nephew of Rama VII, ascended the throne in 1935 but was assasinated under mysterious circumstances in 1946, and his brother Bhumipol Aduldej succeeded him as Rama IX. Under the influence of Phibul's government, the country's name was changed from Siam to Thailand — officially in 1949 — rendered in Thai as *Prathet Thai*.

The Japanese outflanked the Allied troops in Malaya and Burma in 1941 and the Phibul government complied with the Japanese in this action by allowing them into the Gulf of Thailand; consequently the Japanese troops occupied Thailand itself. Phibul then declared war on the US and Great Britain (1942) but Seni Pramoj, the Thai ambassador in Washington, refused to deliver the declaration. Phibul resigned in 1944 under pressure from the Thai underground resistance, and after V-J day in 1945 Seni became premier. In 1946, the year King Ananda was assasinated, Seni and his brother Kukrit were unseated in a general election and a democratic civilian group took power for a short time, only to be overthrown by Phibul in 1948. In 1951 power was wrested from Phibul by General Sarit Thanarat, who continued the tradition of military dictatorship. However, Phibul somehow retained the actual position of premier until 1957 when Sarit finally had him exiled. Elections that same year forced Sarit to resign, go abroad for 'medical treatment', and then return in 1958 to launch another coup. This time he abolished the constitution, dissolved the parliament, and banned all political parties, maintaining effective power until his death in 1963 of cirrhosis. From 1964 to 1973 the Thai nation was ruled by army officers Thanom Kittikachorn and Praphat Charusathien, during which time Thailand allowed the US to develop several army bases within her borders in support of the American campaign in Vietnam.

Reacting to political repression, 10,000 Thai students publicly demanded a real constitution in June 1973. In October of the same year the military brutally suppressed a large demonstration at Thammasat University in Bangkok, but General Krit Sivara and King Bhumiphol refused to support further bloodshed, forcing Thanom and Praphat to leave Thailand. An elected constitutional government ruled until October 1976 when students demonstrated again, this time protesting the return of Thanom to Thailand as a monk. Thammasat University again became a battlefield and a new right-wing government was installed with Thanin Kraivichien as premier. This particular incident really disillusioned many Thai students and older intellectuals not directly involved, with the result that numerous idealists 'dropped out' of Thai society and joined the insurgents in the forests. In October 1977 another coup ousted Thanin and installed Kriangsak. In 1980 the military-backed position changed hands again, leaving Prem at the stern.

If you get the idea that the coup d'etat is popular in Thailand you're on the right track: I've counted 14 successful or attempted coups since 1932 (an average of almost three per decade!), not counting election-forced resignations. There have also been ten 'permanent' constitutions enacted since the first. However, even the successful coups rarely have resulted in drastic change and the Thai commoner will tell you that things *never* change — it depends on how closely you observe politics. Each new leader claims a renewed campaign against the communist threat within Thailand and a stronger defence against the external threat, while sumultaneously promising a liberalization of domestic repression/human rights. Freedom of speech is fairly curtailed in Thailand but appears to be improving slightly and the Bangkok curfew of the Thanin/Kriangsak years has been lifted.

(Anyone who's spent the night in one of Bangkok's mosquito-infested 'detention areas' for being out past curfew will most fully appreciate this.) Every leading political figure must receive the support of the Thai military who are generally staunch reactionaries so we can't expect any miracles in the near future. Considering Thailand's geographic position it's difficult not to understand, to some extent, the fears of this ultra-conservative group. It is a paradoxical situation that can only be worked out by the Thais themselves in cooperation with their South-East Asian neighbours. Visitors to Thailand are advised *not* to become involved in local politics in any way.

RELIGION

About 95% of the Thai citizenry are Theravada Buddhists. The Thais themselves frequently call their religion *Lankavamsa* (Sinhalese lineage) Buddhism because Siam originally received Buddhism during the Sukhothai era from Sri Lanka, whereas strictly speaking (according to Thai scholars), Theravada refers to only the earliest forms of Buddhism practised during the Ashokan and immediate post-Ashokan periods in South Asia. The early Dvaravati and pre-Dvaravati forms of Buddhism are not the same as that which has existed in Siamese territories since the 13th century. Since the Sukhothai period Thailand has maintained an unbroken canonical tradition and 'pure' ordination lineage, the only country among the Theravadin (using Theravada in its doctrinal sense) countries to do so. Ironically, when the ordination lineage in Ceylon broke down during the 18th century under Dutch persecution, it was Siam that restored the Sangha there. To this day the major sect in Sri Lanka is called *Siamopalivamsa* (Siam-Upali lineage, Upali being the name of the Siamese monk who led the expedition to Ceylon), or simply *Siam Nikaya*, the Siamese sect.

Basically, the Theravada school of Buddhism is an earlier, and, (according to its followers), less corrupted form of Buddhism than the Mahayana schools found in East Asia or in the Himalayan lands. The Theravada ('council of the elders') schools is also called the 'southern' school since it took the southern route from India, its place of origin, through South-East Asia (Burma, Thailand, Laos, and Cambodia in this case), while the 'northern' school proceeded north into Nepal, Tibet, China, Korea, Mongolia, Vietnam, and Japan. Because the southern school tried to preserve or limit the Buddhist doctrines to only those canons codified in the early Buddhist era, the northern school gave Theravada Buddhism the name Hinayana, or the 'lesser vehicle'. They considered themselves Mahayana, the 'great vehicle', because they built upon the earlier teachings, 'expanding' the doctrine in such a way so as to respond more to the needs of lay people, or so it is claimed.

Theravada or Hinayana doctrine stresses the three principal aspects of existence, namely *dukkha* (suffering, unsatisfactoriness, dis-ease), *anicca* (impermanency, transiency of all things), and *anatta* (non-substantiality or non-essentiality of reality: no permanent 'soul'). These concepts, when 'discovered' by Siddhartha Gautama in the sixth century BC, were in direct contrast to the Hindu belief in an eternal, blissful, Self or *Paramatman*, hence Buddhism was originally a 'heresy' against India's Brahmanist religion.

Gautama, an Indian prince-turned-ascetic, subjected himself to many years of severe austerities to arrive at this vision of the world, and was given the title Buddha, 'the enlightened' or 'the awakened'. Gautama Buddha spoke of four noble truths which had the power to liberate any human being who could realize them. These four noble truths are:

1 The truth of suffering — 'Existence is suffering'.
2 The truth of the cause of suffering — 'Suffering is caused by desire'.
3 The truth of the cessation of suffering — 'Eliminate the cause of suffering (desire) and suffering will cease to arise'.
4 The truth of the path — 'The eight-fold path is the way to eliminate desire/extinguish suffering'.

The 'eight-fold path' *(athangika-magga)* consists of: (1) right understanding; (2) Right mindedness (or 'right thought'); (3) right speech; (4) right bodily conduct; (5) right livelihood; (6) right effort; (7) right attentiveness; (8) right concentration. These eight limbs belong to three different 'pillars' of practice: morality or *sila* (3-5); concentration or *samadhi* (7-8); and wisdom or *panna* (1-2). Some Buddhists believe the path, called the Middle Way since ideally it avoids both extreme austerity as well as extreme sensuality, is to be taken in successive stages, while others say the pillars and/or limbs are interdependent.

The *summum bonum* of Theravada Buddhism is *nibbana* (Sanskrit: nirvana) which literally means the 'blowing-out' or 'extinction' of all causes of *dukkha*. Effectively it means an end to all corporeal existence whether it be heaven, hell, human, animal, plant, or inanimate existence — an end to that which is forever subject to suffering, and which is conditioned from moment to moment as *karma*, action. In reality, most Thai Buddhists aim for rebirth in a 'better' existence rather than the supramundane goal of nibbana, which is highly misunderstood by Asians as well as westerners. Many Thais express the feeling that they are somehow unworthy of nibbana. By feeding monks, giving donations to temples, and performing regular worship at the local *wat* (temple) they hope to improve their lot, acquiring enough merit (Pali: *punna*; Thai: *bun*) to prevent, at least, lower rebirths. The making of merit *(tham bun)* is an important social as well as religious activity in Thailand. The concept of reincarnation is almost universally accepted in Thailand, even by non-Buddhists, and the Buddhist theory of karma is well-expressed in the Thai proverb '*tham dii, dai dii; tham chua, dai chua*' — 'do good and receive good; do evil and receive evil'.

The *triratna*, or Triple Gems, highly respected by Thai Buddhists, include the Buddha, the Dhamma (the teachings), and the Sangha (the Buddhist brotherhood). Each is quite visible in Thailand. The Buddha in his myriad and omnipresent sculptural form is found on a high shelf in the lowliest roadside restaurants and in the lounges of the expensive Bangkok hotels. The Dhamma is chanted morning and evening in every *wat* and taught to every Thai citizen in primary school. The Sangha is seen everywhere in the presence of orange-robed monks, especially in the early morning hours when they perform their alms-rounds, in what has almost become a travel-guide cliche in motion. Socially, every Thai male is expected to become a monk for a short period in his life, optimally between the time he finishes school and starts a career or marries. Men or boys under 20 years of age may enter the Sangha as novices, and this is not unusual since a family earns great merit when one of its sons takes robe and bowl. Traditionally the length of time spent in the *wat* is three months, during the Buddhist lent (Thai *phansaa*) beginning in July. However, nowadays men may spend as little as a week or fifteen days to accrue merit as monks. There are about 20,000 monasteries in Thailand and 150,000 monks; many of these monks ordain for a lifetime. Of these a large percentage become scholars and teachers, while some specialize in healing and/or folk magic.

The Sangha is divided into two sects, the Mahanikai and the Thammayut. The latter is a minority sect (one Thammayut to 35 Mahanikai) begun by King Mongkut and patterned after an early Mon form of monastic discipline which he had practised as a *bhikkhu*. Generally discipline for Thammayut monks is more strict — for example, they eat only once a day, before noon and must eat only what is in their alms-bowls, whereas Mahanikais eat twice before noon and may accept side dishes. Thammayut monks are expected to attain proficiency in meditation as well as Buddhist scholarship or scripture-study; the Mahanikai monks typically 'specialize' in one or the other.

An increasing number of foreigners come to Thailand to ordain as Buddhist monks, especially to study with the famed meditation masters of the forest *wats* in north-east Thailand.

Recommended books about Buddhism in Thailand:
Buddhism in Transition by Donald K Swearer
Buddhism in the Modern World ed by Heinrich Dumoulin
Buddhism, Imperialism, and War by Trevor Ling
World Conqueror and World Renouncer by Stanley Tambiah
Living Buddhist Masters by Jack Kornfield
Buddhism Explained by Phra Khantipalo

General books about Buddhism:
What the Buddha Taught by Walpola Rahula
The Central Conception of Buddhism by Th Stcherbatsky
Buddhist Dictionary by Mahathera Nyanatiloka

There is an excellent Buddhist bookstore selling English-language books across the street from the main entrance of Wat Bovornives in Bangkok.

Minority Religions

Most of the Malays in the south as well as a small percentage of Thais are followers of Islam, amounting to about 4% of the total population. The remaining 1% are Confucianists, Taoists, Mahayana Buddhists, Christians and Hindus. Muslim mosques (in the south) and Chinese temples are both common enough that you will probably come across some in your travels in Thailand. Before entering *any* temple, sanctuary or mosque you must remove your shoes, and in a mosque your head must be covered.

FESTIVALS & HOLIDAYS

31 January-
1 February

Phra Buddhabaht Fair Annual pilgrimage to the Temple of the Holy Footprint at Saraburi, 236 km north-north-east of Bangkok. Quite an affair, with music, outdoor drama, many other festivities. The shrine is worth visiting even in the 'off-season', if you're in the area.

February

Flower Carnival in Chieng Mai Colourful floats and parades exhibiting Chieng Mai's cultivated flora.

February /
March

Makha Bucha Held on the full moon of the third lunar month to commemorate the preaching of the Buddha to 1250 enlightened monks who came to hear him 'without prior summons'. A public holiday throughout the country culminating in a candlelit circumambulation of the main chapel at every *wat*.

6 April

Chakri Day Public holiday commemorating the founder of the Chakri dynasty, Rama I.

13-15 April

Songkran Festival The New Year's celebration of the lunar year in Thailand. Buddha images are 'bathed', monks and elders receive the respect of younger Thais by the sprinkling of water over their hands, and a lot of water is tossed about for fun. Songkran generally gives everyone a chance to release their frustrations and literally cool off during the peak of the hot season. Hide out in your room or expect to be soaked; the latter is a lot of more fun.

5 May

Coronation Day Public holiday. The King and Queen preside at a ceremony at Wat Phra Kaew in Bangkok, commemorating their 1946 coronation.

May
(Full Moon)

Visakha Bucha Falls on the 15th day of the waxing moon in the sixth lunar month, which is considered the date of the Buddha's birth, enlightenment, and *parinibbana*, or passing away. Activities are centred around the *wat*, with candlelit processions, much chanting and sermonizing, etc. Public holiday.

Mid-July	*Asanha Bucha* Full moon is a must for this holiday, too, commemorating the first sermon preached by the Buddha. Public holiday.
Mid-to-late July	*Kao Phansaa* (beginning of Buddhist 'lent') The traditional time of year for young men to enter the monkhood for the rainy season, and for all monks to station themselves in a single monastery for the three months. A good time to observe a Buddhist ordination. Public holiday.
12 August	*Queens's birthday* Public holiday.
Mid-October to mid-November	*Thawt Kathin* A one month period at the end of 'lent' during which new monastic robes and requisites are offered to the Sangha.
23 October	*Chulalongkorn Day* Public holiday in commemoration of King Chulalongkorn (Rama V).
October-November	*Loi Krathong* On the proper full moon night, small lotus-shaped baskets or boats made of banana leaves containing flowers, incense, candles, and a coin are floated on Thai rivers, lakes and canals. This is a peculiarly Thai festival.
3rd weekend in November	*Annual elephant round-up* in Surin. Pretty touristy these days, but no more so than the 'running of the bulls' in Pamplona, Spain.
5 December	*King's birthday* Public holiday.
31 December-1 January	*New Year's Day* A rather recent public holiday in deference to the western calendar.

Note: The official year in Thailand is reckoned from 543 BC, the beginning of the Buddhist Era, so that 1982 AD = 2525 BE.

ECONOMY

About 76% of Thai labour is engaged in agriculture and only 7% in industry. Thailand's major exports are rice, tapioca, sugar, rubber, maize, tin, cement, pineapple and textiles. Average per capita income by the end of the 70s was US$500 per year, with a GNP growth rate (net) of 6-7%. Travellers should keep in mind that Thailand has quite a high rate of inflation these days (about 25% in Bangkok) — a large bottle of Singh beer that was 15B three or four years ago is 33-35B today. The north-east of Thailand has the lowest inflation rate and cost of living. This region is generally poorer than the rest of the country and doesn't get much tourism; therefore it offers excellent value for the traveller and is well worth a visit — a lot of good silk-weaving is done in the north-east, for example. In the south, fishing, tin mining, and rubber production keep the local economy fairly stable. Central Thailand grows fruit, sugar cane, and rice for export, and supports some industry (textiles, food processing, wood and cement). North Thailand produces mountain or dry rice (as opposed to 'water-rice', the bulk of the crop produced in Thailand) for local use, maize, tea, certain fruits and teak.

ARTS/MUSIC

The following scheme is the standard one used to categorize styles of Thai art, principally sculpture and architecture (since very little painting prior to the 19th century has survived).

Dvaravati style	6th-11th centuries
Srivijaya style	8th-13th centuries
Lopburi style	11th-14th centuries
U Thong style	12th-15th centuries
Sukhothai style	13th-15th centuries
Chieng Saen style	12th-20th centuries
Ayuthaya style	15th-late 18th centuries
Bangkok style	late 18th century to present

A good way to acquaint yourself with these styles, if you are interested, is to visit the National Museum in Bangkok, where works from each of these periods are on display. Then as you travel upcountry and view old monuments and sculpture you'll know what you're seeing, as well as what to look for.

Sites of historical interest for art art and architecture are:

Thonburi	Lamphun
Nakhorn Pathom	Nan
Rajburi	Sukhothai
Ayuthaya	Si Satchanalai
Lopburi	Kampaeng Phet
Chaiya	Sawankhaloke
Chieng Mai	Phitsanuloke
Chieng Saen	Phimai

Recommended books:
Arts of Thailand by A B Griswold
A Concise History of Buddhist Art in Siam by Reginald LeMay

Several good English-language books on Thai art are for sale at the National Museum, also.

Music

From a western perspective, traditional Thai music is some of the most
...re on the planet, and is an acquired taste for most of us. Fortunately

I've acquired it and suggest that it is well worth the effort! The classical stuff is spicy, like Thai food, and features an incredible array of textures and subtleties, hair-raising tempos and pastoral melodies. The classical orchestra is called the *piphat*, and can include as few as five players or more than twenty.

Among the more common instruments is the *pi*, a woodwind instrument which uses a reed mouthpiece, and which is heard prominently at Thai boxing matches. The *pi* is a relative of a similar Indian instrument, as is the *pin*, a banjo-like string instrument descended from the Indian *vina*. A bowed instrument similar to ones played in China and Japan is aptly called the *saw*. The *ranaad ek* is the wooden percussion instrument resembling the western xylophone. An instrument of tuned gongs arranged in a semi-circle is the *gong wong yai*. There are also several different kinds of drums, some played with the hands, some with sticks.

The *piphat* was originally developed to accompany classical dance-drama *(khon)* and shadow theatre *(nang)* but can be heard in straight-forward performance, these days, in temple fairs as well as concerts. One reason classical Thai music may sound strange to the western ear is that it does not use a tempered scale as we have been accustomed to hearing since Bach's time. In fact, they do have an eight-note octave but it is arranged in seven full intervals, with no 'semi-tones'.

In the north and north-east several types of reed instruments with multiple bamboo pipes, functioning basically like a mouth-organ, are popular. Chief among these is the *khaen*, which originated in Laos, and when played by an adept sounds like a rhythmic, churning calliope.

Popular Thai music has been borrowed much from popular American music but still retains a distinct flavour of its own, even though modern Thai musicians may play electric guitars, saxophones, drum kits, and electronic keyboards. Some of the musicians in Bangkok, however, have succeeded in losing all vestiges of Thai tradition in their music, and can play fair copies of everything from Hank Williams to Olivia Newton-John. As far as I have been able to tell, the only good jazz played in Bangkok is played by Filipinos. To me this is ironic since I would put some of the wilder *pi*-players up against John Coltrane anytime!

Recommended books:
The Traditional Music of Thailand by David Morton
Thai Music by Phra Chen Duriyanga

LANGUAGE

During your travels in Thailand, meeting and getting to know Thai people can be a very rewarding experience. I would particularly urge shoestring travellers, young and old, to make the effort to meet Thai college and university students. Thai students are, by and large, eager to meet their peers from other countries. They will often know some English, so communication is not as difficult as it may be with merchants, civil servants, etc, plus they are generally willing to show you useful Thai words and phrases. Learning some Thai is indispensable for travelling in the kingdom; naturally, the more language one picks up, the closer one comes to Thailand's culture and people. Foreigners who speak Thai are so rare in Thailand that it doesn't take much to impress most Thais with a few words in their own language. Don't let laughter at your linguistic attempts discourage you; this amusement is an expression of their appreciation.

Thai is one of the oldest languages in East and South-East Asia; according to linguist/anthropologist Paul Benedict it may even pre-date Chinese, at least in its prototypical form. Many of the so-called 'loan words' thought to be borrowed from Chinese by the Thais, actually have an Austro-Thai origin. At any rate, Chinese and Thai have many similarities, since both are mono-syllabic tonal languages. In Thai the meaning of a single syllable may be altered by means of five different tones (in standard, central Thai): level or mid tone; high tone; low tone; falling tone; and rising tone. Consequently, the syllable *mai*, for example, can mean, depending on the tone, 'new', 'burn', 'wood', 'not?', or 'not'. This makes it rather tricky to learn at first, for those of us who come from more or less non-tonal language traditions. Even when we 'know' what the correct tone in Thai should be, our tendency to denote emotion, verbal stress, the interrogative, etc, through tone modulation, often interferes with speaking the correct tone. So the first rule in learning to speak Thai is to divorce emotions from your speech, at least until you have learned the Thai way to express them without changing essential tone value.

The Thai script, a fairly recent development in comparison with the spoken language (King Ram Khamheng introduced the script in 1283), consists of 44 consonants (but only 21 separate *sounds*) and 48 vowel and diphthong possibilities (32 separate *signs*) and is of Sanskritic origin. Written Thai proceeds from left to right, though vowel-signs may be written before, above, below, 'around' (before, above *and* after), *or* after consonants, depending on the sign. Though learning the alphabet is not difficult, the writing system itself is fairly complex, so unless you are planning a pretty lengthy stay in Thailand it should perhaps be foregone in favour of learning to actually speak the language. At the back of the book is a list of prominent place-names in Thai script as well as Roman, so that you can at least 'read' the names of destinations in a pinch, or point to them if necessary.

For the following phrase section I have used some common English punctuation marks to indicate the corresponding Thai tones. The level or mid tone is pronounced 'flat', at the relative middle of the speaker's vocal range.

The falling tone is pronounced as if we were emphasizing a word, or calling someone's name from afar. Generally in English an exclamation point (!) is used to indicate this kind of stress, so it serves well as a symbol for the falling tone. Example *mai!* = 'no' or 'not'.

The rising tone sounds like the inflection English-speakers generally give to a question — 'You like soup?' — so the question mark (?) will serve for the rising tone. Example *saam?* = 'three'.

The low tone is 'flat' like the mid tone, but pronounced at the relative *bottom* of one's vocal range. Low, level, and with no inflection. Linguists sometimes call it the 'period' tone, so I have used the period mark (.) for its designation. Example: *baat.* = 'Baht' (the Thai currency).

The high tone is usually the most difficult for westerners. It is pronounced near the relative top of the vocal range, as level as possible. I have used the apostrophe mark (') for the high tone. Example: *nii'* = 'this'.

On a visual curve the tones might look something like this:

─	⌒	⌄	─	─
Mid	Falling	Rising	Low	High

Words in Thai that appear to have more than one syllable are usually compounds made up of two or more word units, each with its own tone, or they may be words taken directly from Sanskrit or Pali, in which case each syllable must still have its own tone. Sometimes the tone of the first syllable is not as important as that of the last, so for these I am omitting the tone mark.

Here is a guide to the phonetic system used below.

Consonants

th	t as in English 'tea'
ph	p as in English 'pup'
kh	k as in English 'kite'
k	g as in English 'good' or k in 'cuckoo'
t	like English 't' but unaspirated or 'unexploded'; close to 'd' but unvoiced.
p	similar to 'p' in 'put', unvoiced, unaspirated
ng	as in English 'sing'; used as an initial consonant in Thai

All the remaining consonants correspond closely to their English counter-parts.

Vowels

i	as in English 'it'	eu	as in French 'deux'
ii	as in English 'feet' or 'tea'	eua	diphthong of 'eu' + 'a'
ai	as in English 'pipe' or 'I'	ao	as in English 'now' or 'cow'
aa	long 'a' as in 'father'	aw	as in English 'jaw'
a	half as long as 'aa' above	o	as in English 'phone'
ae	as in English 'bat' or 'tab'	oh	as in English 'toe'
e	as in English 'hen'		
u	as in English 'flute'		
uu	as in English 'food'		

Words & Phrases

When being polite the speaker ends his/her sentence with *khrap'* (for men) or *kha'* (for women). It is the gender of the *speaker* that is being expressed here; it is also the common way to answer 'yes' to a question or show agreement.

greetings	*sawat.dii (khrap'/kha')*
how are you?	*pen yangai*
I'm fine	*sabaay.dii*
you	*khun* (for peers) *thaan!* (for elders, people in authority)
I	*phom?* (for men) *diichan?* (for women)
thank you	*khawp. khun*
do you have ... ?	*...mii mai?* (subject goes first, eg *kuaythiaw? mii mai?* = 'Do you have noodles?')
I, you, he/she/it does not have	*mai! mii*
No	*mai! chai!*
No?	*mai?* or *chai! mai?*
where is ... ?	*...yuu. thii! nai?* (subject first)
when?	*meuarai* (or *meu!arai*)
how much?	*Thao! rai*
It doesn't matter	*mai! pen rai*
how much is this?	*nii' thao! rai* (or *gii baat.*)
What is this?	*nii' arai*
go	*pai*
will go	*ja. bai*
come	*maa*
will come	*ja. maa*
What is your name?	*khun cheu! arai*
My name is ...	*phom? cheu! ...* (men), *diichan? cheu! ...* (women)
(I) like	*chawp! ...*
(I) do not like ...	*mai! chawp! ...*
(I) would like (+ verb)	*yaak. ja.*
(I) would not like	*mai!yaak. ja.*
(I) would like to eat	*yaak. ja. thaan*
(I) would like (+ noun)	*yaak. dai! ...*
I would like a ticket	*yaak. dai! tua?*
I would like to go ...	*yaak. ja. pai ...*
today	*wan nii'*
tomorrow	*prung! nii'*
yesterday	*meua! waan*
too expensive	*phaeng pai*
cheap, inexpensive	*thuuk.*
a little	*nit' nawy.*
I understand	*khao! jai*
Do you understand?	*khao! jai mai?*
I don't understand	*mai! khao! jai*
food (rice)	*khao!*

bathroom	*hawng! nam'*
room	*hawng!*
motorcycle	*rot' motawsai*
train	*rot' fai*
bus	*rot' me*
car	*rot' yon*
hotel	*rohng raem*
station	*sathaa?nii*
post office	*praisanii*
restaurant	*raan' aahaan?*
hospital	*rohng phayaabaan*
hot	*rawn'*
cold	*nao?*
bath/shower	*ap. nam'*
airport	*sanaam? bin*
market	*talaat.*
beach	*haat.*

one	*neung.*	13	*sip.saam?*
two	*sawng?*	14	*sip.sii.*
three	*saam?*	20	*yii!sip.*
four	*sii.*	21	*yii!sip.et.*
five	*haa!*	22	*yii!sip.sawng?*
six	*hok.*	23	*yii!sip.saam?*
seven	*jet.*	30, 40, 50	*saam?sip., sii,sip.,*
eight	*baet.*		*haa!sip*
nine	*kao!*	100	*neung. rawy'*
10	*sip.*	200	*sawng?rawy'*
11	*sip.et.*	300	*saam?rawy'*
12	*sip.sawng?*	1000	*neung. phan*

Your first attempts to speak the language will probably meet with mixed success, but keep trying. When learning new words/phrases, listen closely to the way the Thais themselves use the various tones — it'll catch on quickly.

For expanding your travel vocabulary, I recommend *Robertson's Practical English-Thai Dictionary* since it has a phonetic guide to pronunciation, with tones, and is compact in size. Published by Charles E. Tuttle Co, Suido 1-chome, 2-6, Bunkyo-ku, Tokyo. For more serious language-learners there are Mary Haas' *Thai-English Student's Dictionary* and George McFarland's *Thai-English Dictionary* (the cream of the crop), both published by Stanford University Press, Stanford, California.

Facts for the Visitor

VISAS

Transit visas and tourist visas cost US$5 and three passport photos; they are good for 30 and 60 days respectively. Passengers arriving in Thailand without visa will be granted a 15-day stay, no extension allowed, and proof of onward journey may be required. Non-immigrant visas are good for 90 days, must be applied for in your home country, cost US$15 and are not that difficult to get if you can offer a good reason for your visit. Currently no extension is allowed on either the transit or tourist visa, though it is easy enough to slip across the Malaysian border for a new visa from Penang.

If you need a re-entry visa for an out-and-back trip to Burma or the like, apply at the Immigration Office on Soi Suan Phlu. Cost is 300B.

Bangkok is a good place to collect visas for westward journeys. See Embassies below.

MONEY

$$20 \text{ Baht} = US\$1$$
$$23 \text{ Baht} = A\$1$$
$$46 \text{ Baht} = £1$$

There are 100 satang in 1 baht; coins include 25 and 50 satang pieces, baht in 1B and 5B coins. There are several denominations of paper currency, but anything over a 100B bill is hard to change upcountry.

No more than 500 baht in Thai currency may be legally brought into Thailand by an individual. There is no black market money exchange for baht, so there is no reason to bring in any Thai currency. Banks or legal money-changers offer the best exchange rate within the country. The baht is firmly attached to the American dollar and as stable.

25 satang equals one 'saleng' in colloquial Thai, so if you're quoted a price of 6 saleng in the market, say, for a small bunch of bananas or bag of peanuts, this means 1½B.

COSTS

Food and accommodation, outside of Bangkok, is cheap, and even in Bangkok it's quite low, especially considering the value *vis a vis* other countries in South and South-East Asia.

Legally any traveller arriving in Thailand must have at least these amounts of money, in cash, travellers' cheques, bank draft, or letter of credit, according to visa category:

Non-immigrant visa:	US$500 per person or US$1000 per family
Tourist visa:	US$250 per person or US$500 per family

Transit visa
   or no visa: US$125 per person or US$250 per family

This may be checked if you arrive on a one-way ticket.or if you look as if you're at 'the end of the road'.

Outside of Bangkok budget travellers should be able to get by on 100B or less per day if you really watch your baht, varying, of course, from place to place. With travel experience it can be done for even less, if you live like a Thai of modest means. Add another 35B per day for every beer you drink. In Bangkok there's almost no limit to the amount you *could* spend, but if you live frugally, avoid the tourist ghettos, and ride the public bus system you could get by on the same or just a little bit more. Typically, though, the traveller spends over 100B per day in Bangkok for accommodations — this is generally the absolute minimum for air-conditioning. The noise, heat, and pollution in Bangkok drives many visitors to seek more comfort than they might otherwise need upcountry. Food is somewhat more expensive in Bangkok; however, in Thonburi, where I lived for some time, many dishes are often *cheaper* than they are upcountry, due to the availability of fresh ingredients. Bangkok is the typical 'primate city' cited by sociologists, meaning that most goods produced by the country as a whole end up in Bangkok. The glaring exception is western food, which Bangkok has more of than anywhere else in the kingdom but charges the most for it. Eat only Thai and Chinese food if you're trying to spend as little as possible. And after all, why go to Thailand to eat steak and potatoes?

Good bargaining, which takes practice, is another way to cut costs. Anything bought in a market should be bargained for, as well as accommodation. Some more specific suggestions concerning costs can be found under Accommodation and Things to Buy.

Transportation between cities and within them is very reasonable; again, bargaining can save you a lot of baht. See Getting Around.

CLIMATE

Thailand basically has three more or less distinct seasons: hot (March-June); rainy (July-October), and cool/dry (November-February). Some people say the rainy season begins in June, some say in July. The truth is it depends on the monsoons in any given year; 'officially' the rains begin in July. It rains more and longer in the south, so that the wet season effectively lasts through January. The temperature is more even all year-round in the south also; when it is 35°C. In Bangkok it may be only 32°C in Phuket. The hot season is the hottest in the north-east plain, easily reaching 37°C in the daytime, and only a few degrees less at night. Most of Thailand is very humid, the mountains in the north being the exception. The temperature can drop to 13°C at night during the cool season in Chieng Mai — if you're visiting the north during the cooler months, long-sleeved shirts and pullovers would be in order.

In central Thailand it rains the most during August and September, though there may be more floods in October since the ground has reached full saturation by then. If you are in Bangkok in early October don't be surprised if you find yourself in hip-deep water in certain parts of the city. It rains a little less in the north, August being the peak month. The northeast gets a bit less rain and periodically suffers droughts. In Phuket it rains most in May (average 21 out of 30 days) and in October (22 out of 30), undergoing two monsoons. Generally travelling in the rainy season is not unpleasant at all, but unpaved roads may close down occasionally.

Best overall time to visit Thailand would be between November and February — during these months it rains least and is not so hot. See the south during the coolest months, December and January, the north in February when it begins warming up, elsewhere (Bangkok included) in November. Of course, if you can't choose your time so carefully, come anytime, but be prepared to roast in April, and to do some wading in September/October. There is a bit of an increase in the total number of tourists in Thailand during the optimum months.

HEALTH

There are no health requirements for Thailand in terms of required vaccinations unless you are coming from an infected area. Travellers should have a cholera immunization prior to arriving, nonetheless; if a cholera epidemic breaks out you won't have to receive an injection through a questionable needle at a temporary roadside health centre. Tetanus booster would be a good idea, too, in case you injure yourself while travelling. You should also check if vaccinations are required by any countries you are going to after visiting Thailand.

As with any Asian country, care should be taken in consuming food or drink. Besides malaria, really serious diseases are not too common in Thailand. Bacteriological dysentery, or traveller's diarrhoea, strikes most visitors who stay for any length of time outside of Bangkok. Thai soft drinks are safe to drink, as is the weak Chinese tea served in most restaurants. Ice is probably not safe, but is very difficult to resist in the hot season. It is best to buy fruit that you can peel and slice yourself (cheaper, too), but most fare at foodstalls is reasonably safe.

Malaria suppresants should be taken during and after one's visit to Thailand. This mosquito-carried disease is on the increase all over the country and most of the strains are chloroquine-resistant, including the deadly *Plasmodium falciparum*. Taking a few simple precautions can greatly reduce your chances of contracting any kind of malaria. First, the best malaria suppresent to take is Fansidar, which seems to be available just about everywhere except in the US. Fansidar can be bought, however, in Thailand if you are coming from the States. Persons allergic to sulphonamides should not take Fansidar; otherwise, no adverse reactions have been reported. A good mosquito repellant called Skeetolene is sold in Thailand (manufactured by the British Dispensary in Bangkok), to be applied to skin and clothes, and mosquito coils do an excellent job of repelling mosquitoes in your room. Day mosquitoes do not carry malaria, so it is only in the night that you have to worry — the day variety do carry some six strains of dengue fever, but dengue is not so dangerous an affliction, usually subsiding after a few days.

There are several good hospitals in Bangkok and Chieng Mai:

Bangkok:
   Bangkok Christian Hospital, 124 Silom Rd. Tel 2336981-9.
   Seventh Day Adventist Hospital, 430 Phitsanuloke Rd.
   Ramathibodi Hospital, Rama VI Rd. Tel 2813566, 2811364, 2819110, 2819110, 2811616.

Chieng Mai:
   McCormick Hospital, Nawarat Rd.
   Ariawongse Clinic, Changmoi Rd.
   Chieng Mai Hospital, Suan Dawk Rd.

ACCOMMODATION
Places to stay are abundant, varied, and reasonably priced in Thailand.

Hostels, Guest Houses, YMCA/YWCA's
These are generally the cheapest accommodation but they are not found everywhere in Thailand. There are ten hostels and guest houses in Bangkok, including the two Y's, at this writing, one Y in Chieng Mai (but *many* guest houses and youth hostels), and one official Thai Youth Hostel in each of the following towns: Ayuthaya, Chieng Mai, Chonburi, Kanchanaburi, Lopburi, Nakhorn Nayok, Nakorn Pathom, Nakhorn Sawan, Phitsanuloke, and Saraburi. The rates for the latter range from 20 to 30 baht per night, depending on your age, and accommodation is usually dormitory style. All either serve meals or can arrange for them. Guest houses vary quite a bit in daily rates and facilities. Chieng Mai has a particularly good selection of guest houses while Bangkok has only a handful. YMCA/YWCA's provide generally very comfortable accommodations but you have to pay for it.

Chinese-Thai Hotels
The standard Thai hotels, often run by Chinese-Thai families, are the easiest accommodations to come by and generally are very reasonable in rates. They may be located on the main street of town and/or near bus and train stations. The most economical ones to stay in are those without air-conditioning; typical rooms are clean and include a double bed and a ceiling fan, some have attached Thai-style bathrooms (this will cost you a little more). Rates may or may not be posted; if not, they may be increased for the *farang*, so it is worthwhile to try bargaining. It is best to have a look

around before agreeing to check in, to make sure the room *is* clean, that the fan and lights work, etc. If there is any problem request another room or a good discount.

Some of these hotels may double as brothels; the perpetual traffic in and out can be a bit noisy but is generally bearable. The best (cheapest) hotels have Thai or Chinese names posted in the scripts of both languages (newer hotels may have the name in Romanised script as well), but you will learn how to find and identify them with experience. Most of these hotels can arrange to have food served to you downstairs, and there are often restaurants and noodle-shops nearby.

Government-owned Guest Houses/Bungalows
At Poo Kradung National Park near Loei and at Khao Yai National Park near Nakhorn Nayok there are government-owned guest houses/bungalows, very nice, with moderate to high rates (200-1000B). Other government accommodation is available near the Sukhothai old city ruins.

Universities/Schools
College and university campuses may be able to provide inexpensive accommodation during the summer vacation (March-June). Outside of Bangkok there are teacher's colleges in almost every sizeable town in Thailand, called *withayalai khru* in Thai, and there are universities in Chieng Mai, Nakhorn Pathom, Khon Kaen, Mahasarakham, and Songkhla.

Tourist Class Hotels
These are found only in the main tourist destinations: Chieng Mai, Bangkok, Pattaya, Songkhla, Phuket, Hat Yai, plus a few in towns near former US military bases: Tak, Udorn, and Sattaheep. They start at around 300B, outside of Bangkok and Chieng Mai, and proceed to 1000B or more — genuine tourist class hotels in Bangkok start at 500B or so and go to 2000B if you can pay it. These will all have air-con and western-style toilets.

Temples
If you are a Buddhist or can make a good show of it, you may be able to stay overnight in some temples for a small donation. Facilities may be very basic, though, and early rising is expected. Usually for men only, unless the *wat* has a place for lay women to stay. In addition the World Fellowship of Buddhists (33 Sukhumwit Rd) has a list of several meditation *wats* around the country that will accommodate lay students for periods of several weeks if you are interested.

FOOD
Some people take to the food in Thailand immediately while others don't; Thai dishes can be pungent and spicy — a lot of garlic and chilis are used, especially *phrik kii noo*, or 'mouse-shit peppers'. These are the small

torpedo-shaped devils which can be pushed aside if you are timid about 10-alarm curries. Almost all Thai food is cooked with fresh ingredients, including vegetables, poultry, pork, and some beef. And plenty of rice, lime juice, lemon grass, and fresh coriander leaf are added to give the food its characteristic tang, and fish sauce (generally made from anchovies), or shrimp paste to make it salty. Other common seasonings include 'laos' root (Thai: *khaa*), black pepper, ground peanuts (more often a condiment), tamarind juice (*nam makhaam*), ginger (*khing*), and coconut milk (*kati*). The Thais eat a lot of what could be called Chinese food, too, which is generally, but not always, less spicy. In the north and north-east 'sticky' or glutinous rice is common and is traditionally eaten with the hands.

Restaurants or foodstalls outside of Bangkok usually do not have menus, so it is worthwhile memorizing a standard 'repertoire' of dishes. Most provinces have their own local specialties in addition to the standards and you might try asking for 'whatever is good', allowing the proprietors to choose for you. Of course, you might get stuck with a large bill this way, but with a little practice in Thai social relations you may get some very pleasant results. The most economical places to eat, and the most dependable, are noodle-shops and night markets. Most towns and villages have at least one night market and several noodle-shops. The night market(s) in Chieng Mai have a slight reputation for over-charging (especially for large parties), but on the other hand I have never been over-charged for food anywhere in Thailand. It helps if you speak Thai as much as possible.

At the back of the book is a list of standard dishes in Thai script with a transliterated pronunciation guide using the system outlined in the Language section, and English translation/description.

Thai food is served with a variety of condiments, including ground red pepper, ground peanuts, vinegar with sliced peppers, fish sauce with peppers (*nam plaa phrik*), a spicy red sauce called *nam phrik si raachaa* (from Si Racha, of course), and any number of other special sauces for particular dishes. Soy sauce (*nam sii-yu*) can be requested.

Except for the 'rice plates' and noodle dishes, Thai meals are usually ordered family style, which is to say that two or more people order together, sharing different dishes. Traditionally, the party orders one of each kind of dish, eg one chicken, one fish, one soup, etc. One dish is generally enough for two people. One or two extras may be ordered for a large party. If you come to eat at a Thai restaurant alone and order one of these 'entrees', you had better be hungry or know enough Thai to order a small portion. This latter alternative is not really too acceptable socially; Thais generally consider eating alone in a restaurant unusual. But then as a *farang* you're an exception anyway.

Thais eat with a fork and spoon, except for noodles which are eaten with spoon and chopsticks (*ta-kiap*), and sticky rice, which is rolled into balls and eaten with hands, along with the food accompanying it.

THINGS TO BRING

As little as possible — one medium-size shoulder bag or backpack should do it. Pack light, wash-and-wear, natural-fabric clothes, unless you're going to be in the north in the cool season, in which case you should have a sweater/pullover. Pick up a *phakama* (short Thai-style sarong for men) or *phasin* (same made for women but longer) to wear in your room, on the beach, or when bathing outdoors. These can be bought at any local market (different patterns/colours in different parts of the country) and the sellers will show you how to tie them. The *phakama/phasin* is a very handy item, it can be used to sleep on or as a light bedspread, as a make-shift 'shopping bag', as a turban-scarf to keep off the sun & absorb perspiration, as a towel, as a small hammock, and as a device with which to climb coconut palms — to name just a few of its many functions. (It is not considered proper street attire, however.)

Sunglasses are a must for most people, they can be bought cheaply in Bangkok. Slip-on shoes or sandals are highly recommended — besides being cooler than tie shoes, they are easily removed before entering a Thai home or temple. A small flashlight is a good idea, makes it easier to find your way back to your bungalow at night if you are staying at the beach or at a government guest house. Sunscreen and mosquito repellent can be purchased in Thailand, as can toothpaste, soap and most other toiletries.

PHOTOGRAPHY

Film is expensive in Thailand so bring enough to last throughout your visit. Also it is best to wait until you return home to have film processed, as the Thais are not known for their excellence in non-commercial film-processing. Pack some silica gel with your camera to prevent mould from growing on the inside of your lenses. Hill tribespeople in some of the more visited areas expect money if you photograph them, while certain Red Karens will not allow you to point a camera at them.

A polarising filter could be useful to cut down on tropical glare at certain times of day, particularly around water or highly-polished glazed tilework. Keep an eye on your camera — they are very expensive in Thailand and are thus tempting to thieves.

THINGS TO BUY

There are a lot of good bargains awaiting you in Thailand if you have the space to carry them back.

Fabrics Possibly the best all-around buy in Thailand, in my opinion. Thai silk is considered the best in the world and can be purchased cheaply in the north-east where it is made or, more easily, in Bangkok. Excellent and reasonably-priced tailor shops can make your choice of fabric into almost any pattern. Cottons are also a good deal — common items like the *phakama*, which is reputed to have over a hundred uses in Thailand, and the *phasin*, the slightly larger female equivalent, make great tablecloths and curtains. Good ready-made cotton shirts are available (ie the *maw hawm*   Thai work shirt, and the *kuay haeng* – 'Chinese' style shirt), see the sections on Pasang in the north and Koh Yaw in the south. Nice batik is available, too. Always haggle on these items.

Shoulder-bags Thai shoulder bags, or *yaams*, are generally quite well made. The *yaam* comes in many varieties, some woven by hill tribes, others by Thai cottage industry. Chieng Mai has a good selection, but Bangkok has the best prices – try the Indian district (Pahurat) for these as well as anything else made of cloth.

Antiques Real antiques cannot be taken out of Thailand without a permit from the Department of Fine Arts. No Buddha image, new or old, may be exported without permission – refer to Fine Arts again, or, in some cases, the Department of Religious Affairs, under the Ministry of Education. Too many private collectors smuggling and hording Siamese art (Buddhas in particular) around the world have caused this situation to arise.

Chinese and Thai antiques are sold in Chinatown in an area called Wang Burapha – the streets with Chinese 'gates' over the entrance. Some antiques (and many fakes) are sold at the Weekend Market, Sanam Luang. Objects for sale in the tourist antique shops are fantastically over-priced, as can be expected.

Jewellery If you know what you are doing, you can make some really good buys, in unset gems as well as finished jewellery. Gold is sold at a good rate; jade, sapphires, and rubies, are the best bargains, though. Buy from reputable dealers only, unless you're a gemologist. I've heard of *farangs* who have really scored big in gem-buying, but be careful. Shop around.

Hill-tribe crafts Interesting embroidery, clothing, bags, some jewellery, all from the north, can be bought in Bangkok at Narayan Phand, a store on Larn Luang Rd, at the Queen's Hillcrafts Foundation in the Sapatum Palace compound behind Siam Centre, and at various tourist shops around town. If you're lucky enough to be in Bangkok at the right time during the hot season, you can attend the great annual hillcrafts sale at the International School off Sukhumvit – quite a crowd turns out for this one since selection and prices can be unusually good, though it seems to vary from year to year. In Chieng Mai there are shops selling handicrafts all along Thapae Rd and there is a shop sponsored by missionaries near Prince Royal College. There is a branch of the Queen's Hillcrafts Foundation in Chieng Rai. It is worthwhile to shop around for the best prices and bargain.

Lacquerware Thailand produces some good Burmese-style lacquerware, and sells some of the Burmese stuff itself, along the northern Burmese border.

Try towns like Mae Sot and Mae Hong Son for the best values.

BATHING IN THAILAND

Upcountry the typical Thai bathroom consists of a tall earthen water jar fed by a spigot, and a plastic or metal bowl. You bathe by scooping water out of the water jar and sluicing it over the body. It's very refreshing during the hot and rainy seasons, but takes a little stamina during the cool season if you're not used to it. If the 'bathroom' has no walls, or if you are bathing at a public well or spring in an area where there are no bathrooms, you should bathe while wearing the *phakama* or *phasin*; bathing nude would offend the Thais.

Which brings me to:

Nudity on Beaches

Regardless of what the Thais may (or may not) have been accustomed to centuries ago, they are quite offended by public nudity today. Bathing nude at beaches in Thailand is illegal. If you are at a truly deserted beach and are sure no Thais may come along, there's nothing stopping you — however, at most beaches (Phuket, etc) travellers should be suitably attired. Recently, when staying in Phuket for an extended period (Kata-Karon-Naiharn area), I talked with a few Thai bungalow/restaurant proprietors who said that nudity on the beaches was what bothered them most about foreign travellers. These Thais took nudity as a sign of disrespect on the part of the travellers for the locals, rather than as a libertarian symbol or modern custom. I was even asked to make signs that they could post forbidding or discouraging nudity — I declined, forgoing a free bungalow for my stay. Thais are extremely modest in this respect (despite racy billboards in Bangkok), and it should not be the traveller's purpose to 'reform' them.

INFORMATION & EMBASSIES

The Tourist Authority of Thailand has several offices within the country and others overseas.

In Thailand
4 Ratchadamnoen Nok Avenue, Bangkok 1, Thailand, Tel 2821143-7

135 Praisani Rd, Chieng Mai, Tel 235334

Saengchoto Rd, Kanchanaburi, Tel 51 1200

53/1-4 Mukkhamontri Rd, Nakhorn Ratchasima, Tel 243427

Chai Hat Rd, Pattaya Beach, Chonburi, Tel 418750

9 Prachatipat Rd, Songkhla, Tel 243747

A Freshly made Buddhas in Sukhothai
B Golden Buddha at Wat Traimit, Bangkok
C Fasting Buddha at Wat U Mong, Chieng Mai

Tourist Authority of Thailand
Overseas Offices

Australia:	12th Floor, Exchange Bldg, Pitt & Bridge St, Sydney NSW 2000, Tel: 277540, 277549
France:	c/o Royal Thai Embassy, 8 Rue Greuze 75116, Paris, Tel 7043221
Japan:	Hibiya Mitsui Bldg, 1-2 Yrakucho 1-chome, Chiyoda-ku, Tokyo 100, Tel: (03) 5806776
Singapore:	c/o Royal Thai Embassy, 370 Orchard Rd, Tel 372158
UK:	9 Stafford Ct, London W1X 3FE, Tel: 4997670, 4997679
USA (east):	5 World Trade Ctr, Suite 2449, New York, NY 10048, Tel 4320433
USA (west):	3400 Wilshire Blvd, Suite 1101, Los Angeles, California, 90010
West Germany:	4th floor Bethmann Strasse, 58/Ecke Kaiserstrasse. 15, 6000 Frankfurt/M. 1. Tel: 0611-295704-295804

EMBASSIES

Australia
7th floor, Thaniya Bldg.
64 Silom Rd.
Tel: 2335970-9
Hours: 8 am-12.30 pm,
1-45 pm-4.30 pm.

Bangladesh
4th floor, Phatra Tanakit Bldg.
183 Sukhumvit Rd.
Tel: 2524059 X-145, 149
Hours: 8.30 am-12.30 pm,
1 pm-4.30 pm

Belgium
44 Soi Phya Phipat, Silom Rd.
Tel: 2330840, 2330841
Hours: 8.30 am-1.30 pm

Britain
1031 Ploenchit Rd.
Tel: 2527160-9
Hours: 8 am-12.30 pm, 2pm-4.30 pm
Wednesday: 8 am-4 pm.

Burma:
132 Sathorn Neua Rd.
Tel: 2332237, 2342258
Hours: 8.30-12.30 pm, 1 pm-4.30 pm
(Monday-Thursday)
8.30 am-12 noon, 1 pm-5 pm (Friday)

Canada
11th floor, Boonmit Bldg.
138 Silom
Tel: 2341651-8
Hours: 8 am-12.30 pm, 1.30-4.30 pm

China
Capital Mansion,
1371 Phaholyothin Rd.
Tel: 2797076-9

Denmark
10 Soi Attakarn Prasit
Sathorn Tai Rd.
Tel 2863930, 2863932
Hours: 8 am-1.30 pm

A Brahma Shrine at the Erawan Hotel, Bangkok
B Wat Arun, Temple of the Dawn, Thonburi
C 13th-century chedi, Wat Chedi Luang, Chieng Saen

France
Customs House Lane
Tel: 2340950-6
Hours: 8.30 am-1 pm, 2.30 pm-5 pm;
Wednesday 8.30 am-1 pm

(West) Germany
9 Sathorn Tai Rd.
Tel: 2964223-7
Hours: 8 am-1 pm

India
139 Pan Rd.
Tel: 2335065
Hours: 8.30 am-12.30 pm, 1 pm-
4.30 pm

Indonesia
600-602 Petchburi Rd.
Tel: 2523135-40
Hours: 7.30 am-12 pm, 1 pm-4 pm.

Japan
1674 New Petchburi Rd.
Tel: 2526151-9
Hours: 8.30 am-12 noon

Korea
6th floor Praparwit Bldg
28/1 Surasak Rd
Tel: 2340723-6
Hours: 8.30-12 noon, 2 pm-5 pm

Laos (Embassy of the Lao People's
Democratic Republic)
193 Sathorn Tai Rd.
Tel 2960010, 2863362
Hours: 8 am-12 noon, 2 pm-4.30 pm

Malaysia
35 Sathorn Tai Rd.
Tel: 2861390-2
Hours: 8.30 am-12.30 pm, 2 pm-
4.30 pm

Nepal
189 Soi Puengsuk, Sukhumvit
Tel: 3917240
Hours: 8 am-12 noon, 1.30 pm-
4.30 pm

Netherlands
106 Withayu Rd.
Tel: 2526103-5
Hours: 8 am-2.30 pm; Tuesday
8 am-12.30 pm, 2 pm-5 pm

New Zealand
The Anglo-Thai Corporation
64 Silom Rd
Tel 2345935
Hours: 8 am-12 noon, 1.30 pm-4
pm

Norway
20th Floor Chokechai
Inter Bldg, 690 Sukhumvit
Tel: 3921164, 3921160

Pakistan
31 Soi Nana Neua 3 Sukhumvit
Tel: 2527036-8
Hours: 8 am-3.30 pm

Philippines
760 Sukhumvit Rd
Tel 3910008, 3910211
Hours: 8 am-12 noon, 1 pm-5 pm

Singapore
129 Sathorn Tai Rd.
Tel: 286211, 1861434
Hours: 8.30 am-12 noon, 1 pm-4.30
pm

Sri Lanka
7th Floor, Nailert Bldg
87 Sukhumvit Rd
Tel 2518534
Hours: 8.30-12 noon, 1 pm-4.45 pm

Sweden
9th floor, Silom Bldg,
197/1 Silom
Tel: 2342891, 2860295
Hours: 8 am-1 pm

Switzerland
35 Withayu Neua Rd
Tel: 2528992-4
Hours: 8 am-4 pm

USA
  95 Withayu Rd,
  Tel: 2525040-9
  Hours: 7.30-12 noon, 1 pm-4.30 pm

USSR
  108 Sathorn Neua Rd,
  Tel 2340824, 2342012
  Hours: 7.30 am-4.15 pm; Monday
  7.30 am-4.15 pm.

Vietnam
  83/1 Withayu Rd,
  Tel 2517203, 2515836-7
  Hours: 8.30 am-4.30 pm (Monday-
  Saturday)

BOOKS & BOOKSHOPS

Two travel guides with some good stuff on history, culture, art, etc are *Nagel's Encyclopedia-Guide to Thailand,* an expensive little book published in Switzerland and *Discovering Thailand* by Clarac and Smithies. The *Insight Guide to Thailand* (Apa Productions, Singapore) is beautifully appointed and well-written although it's a little hefty to carry around as a travel guide — a worthy item for travel guide collectors at any rate.

If you can get hold of a copy of *Hudson's Guide to Chieng Mai and the North* you'll learn a lot about this area that is unknown to the average traveller. Some of the information is out of date (since the book is out of print) but it makes interesting reading and has the best Thai phrase section of any guide published — 218 phrases *with* tone marks. (Phrase sections without tone marks are next to worthless.)

If you are interested in detailed info on hill tribes, get *The Hill Tribes of Northern Thailand* by Gordon Young (Monograph No 1, The Siam Society). Young was born among Lahu tribespeople of third-generation Christian missionaries, speaks several tribal dialects, and is even an honorary Lahu chieftain with the highest Lahu title, the 'Supreme Hunter'. The monograph covers sixteen tribes, including descriptions, photographs, tables, and maps.

Additional serious reading: *The Indianized States of South-East Asia* by George Coedes — classic work on South-East Asian history; and *The Thai Peoples* by Erik Seidenfaden.

The three best bookshops in Bangkok are Asia Books, Sukhumwit Rd, Soi 15; Chalermnit, Erawan Arcade, Ploenchit Rd; DK (Duang Kamol) Bookstore, Siam Square.

NEWSPAPERS

There are four English-language newspapers available in Bangkok and Chieng Mai: *Bangkok Post, Nation* (morning), and *Bangkok World, International Herald Tribune* (afternoon).

Getting There

BY AIR

The expense of getting to Bangkok, per air kilometre, varies quite a bit depending on your point of departure. However, you can take heart in the fact that Bangkok is the cheapest city in the world to fly out of, due to the Thai government's loose restrictions on air fares and the close competition between airlines/travel agencies. The result is that, with a little shopping around, you can come up with some real bargains. If you can find a cheap one-way ticket to Bangkok, take it, because you are virtually guaranteed to find one of equal or lesser cost for the return trip, once you get there.

From most places around the world your best bet will be budget, excursion, or Apex (advance purchase) fares — in inquiring from airlines ask for the various fares in that order. Each carries its own set of restrictions and it's up to you to decide which set works best in your case. Fares are going up and down with regularity these days, but in general they are cheaper September through April than during the rest of the year.

Fares listed below should serve as a guideline — don't count on them staying this way for long (they may go down!).

From Australia The cheapest regular fares are Advance Purchase tickets which range from A$496 to 633 one-way from the Australian east coast to Bangkok depending on the season. Return Apex fares range from A$710 to 974. It is possible to find one-way tickets down to around A$380 by asking around likely travel agents.

From Europe London 'bucket shops' will have tickets to Bangkok available from around £170 one-way or £280 return. It's also easy to stop-over in Bangkok between London and Australia with fares from around £330 to the Australian east coast. Good travel agents to try for these sort of fares are Trail Finders on Earls Court Rd or STA on Old Brompton Rd. Or you can simply check the travel ads in *Time Out* or the *Australasian Express*.

From North America If you can fly from the West Coast, you can get some great deals. First and foremost among the bargains is OC Tours, 800 Airport Blvd, Burlingame, California, 94010 (tel 800-227-5083 outside California, 415-348-6300 in California). OC Tours is a Chinese operated corporation which mainly serves the heavy Chinese traffic between San Francisco and Hong Kong. They even put out an interesting monthly newspaper which is the 'largest trilingual monthly in America' (English, Chinese, Japanese), and which contains a full listing of routes (extensive) and fares (quite low). Their twice weekly flights out of SFO fly World Airways 747s to HK, connecting with Singapore Airlines to Bangkok. Return is SIA again to Hong Kong and China Airlines to SFO. This flight is US$769 round-trip and can be taken out of Los Angeles for the same price. You are allowed a stopover in Hong Kong if you like and the ticket is good for a year. Restrictions: full payment must be in 30 days in advance and there are cancellation penalties involved. A peak season charge of US$30 is added for budget fares. OC Tours can also arrange flights from New York, Chicago, Vancouver, Toronto, Boston, and Washington DC for US$100-200 extra.

Other airways to check, all cheapest from the West Coast, are: Thai International, China Airlines, Korean Air Lines, Pan Am, and World Airways. Each of these has a budget and/or 'super Apex' fare that runs US$850-1000 round-trip from Los Angeles, San Francisco, or Seattle. Thai International offers the best all-around service, both in terms of flight departures and in-flight facilities/food/entertainment. Several of these airlines also fly out of New York and Chicago — tack on US$100-200 to their lowest fares.

From Asia There are regular flights to Bangkok from every major city in Asia and it's not so tricky dealing with inter-Asia flights as most airlines offer about the same fares. Here is a sample of current estimated fares:

Singapore-Bangkok	US$200
Hong Kong-Bangkok	US$140
Kuala Lumpur-Bangkok	US$100
Taipei-Bangkok	US$243
Calcutta-Bangkok	US$125-150 (shop around)
Kathmandu-Bangkok	US$160
Colombo-Bangkok	US$250
New Delhi-Bangkok	US$280
Manila-Bangkok	US$300+ (shop around)

Don Muang International Airport

Don Muang Airport is 25 km north of Bangkok and there are several ways of getting from this concrete monstrosity to the city. Taxis will ask an outrageous amount to transport you to your destination but will usually go for a hundred baht or so, not too bad if you're looking for the fastest way in, or have a few other travellers with whom to share the fare. Taxis flagged down on the highway that pass in front of the airport are cheaper — 50-75B.

Thai Airways has a mini-bus that goes to most major hotels (or some minor ones if the driver feels like it) for 70B per person.

Cheapest of all are the public buses which stop on the highway to Bangkok, out front. The ordinary No. 29 bus is only 3B but often crowded — it comes straight down Phahonyothin Rd after entering the city limits, and this road soon turns into Phayathai Rd, meanwhile passing Phetburi Rd (where you'll want to get off to change buses if you're going to the Democracy Monument area), Rama I Rd (for buses out Sukhumvit, or to walk to the Star Hotel, Reno Hotel, or Muangphol Lodging), and finally turning right on Rama IV Rd to go to the Hualamphong district (where Bangkok's main railway station is located) — you'll want to go the opposite way on Rama IV for the Malaysia, Boston Inn, etc.

The air-conditioned public bus No. 4 also can be boarded at the airport. for 15B to most destinations in Bangkok; it costs less if you're getting off in north Bangkok (say, for the Liberty Hotel in Saphan Khwai district) though this must be established before you pay the fare. Unless you're really strapped for baht, it's worth the extra 12B for the air-con and almost guaranteed seating on the No. 4, especially in the hot season, since the trip downtown by bus can take an hour or more. The No. 4 bus does a route parallel to the No. 29 — down Mitthaphap Rd to Ratchprarop/Ratchadamri Rd, crossing Phetburi, Rama I, Ploenchit, and Rama IV Rds, then down Silom, left on Charoen Krung, and across the river to Thonburi. You ought to have some kind of map of Bangkok before attempting the buses so you'll know approximately where to get off.

Taxis going to the airport from Bangkok generally ask for more fare than taxis coming back — count on 25-50B more. Consider the No. 4 bus.

Airport departure tax is now 50B.

BY LAND
Trains, buses, and taxis enter Thailand from Malaysia, either from the western point of entry, Padang Besar, or the eastern, Sungai Kolok. See the section on south Thailand for train fares between Bangkok and Singapore, Bangkok and Butterworth, etc.

There is currently no land passage allowed between Burma and Thailand (legally), and likewise for Cambodia and Laos, although we can look for Laos to open up in the near future at the Vientiane crossing.

Getting Around

BANGKOK

Here you can save a lot of money by sticking to the public buses, which are 1.50B for any journey under 10 km, although the tickets read 2B. In 1980 when the fare was raised to 2B by the government, mass protest broke out in Bangkok, bringing the fare down to the 1.50B compromise. The fare is 3B for journeys over 10 km, for example from Chulalongkorn University to Bangmot district in Thonburi on Bus No. 21. To do any serious bus-riding you'll need a Bangkok bus map — easiest to read is the one put out by Suwannachai (*Latest Tour's Guide to Bangkok & Thailand*) which also has a decent map of the whole country on the flip side. The bus numbers are clearly marked in red, air-con buses in larger types. Don't expect the routes to be 100% correct, a few have changed since the map came out last, but it'll get you where you're going most of the time. This map usually retails for 30B but can be purchased at the TAT office in Bangkok for 15B.

Taxis in Bangkok have meters but the drivers do not use them. The fare must be decided before you get in the cab unless you really want to get taken for a ride. Fares to most places within central Bangkok should not exceed 25B — add 5B if it's rush hour or after 11 pm. Short distances should be under 20B — Siam Square to Silom Rd, for example, should be around 15B in relatively light traffic. To get these fares you must bargain well. There is an over-supply of taxis in Bangkok so just wave a driver on if he won't meet a reasonable fare and flag down another cab. It gets easier with practice and better results are obtained if you speak some Thai. Petrol prices are high in Thailand and rising, though, so do don't be too hard on the drivers. Better to take a bus if you are really counting pennies; save the taxi for when you're in a genuine hurry.

Tuk-tuks, the three-wheeled taxis that sound like power saws gone berserk, are good only for very short distances. For longer distances they may charge more than the four-wheel variety, and there have been some instances of *tuk-tuk* drivers robbing their fares at night. Bangkok residents often talk of the *tuk-tuks* as a nuisance, even a menace, to their already suffering environment, and some have been trying to get a ban on *tuk-tuks* enacted. A few years ago the city supposedly forbade the further production of any new three-wheel taxis, but on a recent trip there I saw more than a few brand new ones. It's a bit of a moral dilemma, actually, since the *tuk-tuk* drivers are usually poor north-easterners who can't afford to rent the quieter, less polluting Toyota auto-taxis.

Cars and motorcycles can easily be rented in Bangkok if you can afford it and have steel nerves. Rates are around 300B per day, less for a motorcycle, not including insurance. An International Driver's Licence and passport are required. Here are the names and addresses of a few car rents:

Bangkok Car Rent
83/2 Witthayu Rd
tel 252-9729

Choke Dee Car Rent
2/6 Soi 30 Sukhumwit Rd
tel 392-2082

Siam Car Rent
45-49 Sukhumwit Rd
tel 251-1850

New First Car Rent
1 Sukhumwit Soi 1
tel 392-4422

There are several more car rental agencies along Witthayu Rd — many of these rent motorcycles, too.

TRAINS

The railway network in Thailand, run by the Thai government, is surprisingly good. After travelling several thousand miles by train and bus, I have to say that the train wins hands down as the best form of public transport in the kingdom. It is not possible to take the train everywhere in Thailand but if it were that's how I'd go. If you travel third class, the train is also often the cheapest way to cover a long distance; by second class it's about the same as a 'tour bus' but much safer and more comfortable. The trains take a bit longer than a chartered bus, but, on overnight trips especially, it is worth the extra time it takes. There are many advantages that trains offer. There is more space, more room to breathe and stretch out, even in third class, than there is on the best buses. The windows are big and usually open, so that there is no glass between you and the scenery — good for taking photos — and more to see; the scenery itself is always better along the rail routes compared to the scenery along Thai highways — the train regularly passes small villages, farmland, old temples, etc. Decent, reasonably priced food is available and served at your seat. The pitch-and-roll of the railway cars is much easier on the bones, muscles, and nervous system than the quick stops and starts, the harrowing turns, and the pot-hole jolts endured on buses. The train is safer in terms of both accidents en route and robberies. Last, but certainly not least, you meet a lot more interesting people on the trains, or so it seems to me.

There are four main rail lines, the Northern, Southern, North-eastern, and Eastern routes, with several side routes, notably between Nakhorn Pathom and Nam Tok (stopping in Kanchanaburi) in the west central region, between Tung Song and Kan Tang (stopping in Trang) in the south, and between Hat Yai and Songkhla in the south. The Southern line splits at Hat Yai, one route going to Sungai Kolok in Malaysia, through Yala, one route going to Padang Besar in the west, also on the Malaysian border.

The disadvantage of riding trains, in addition to the time factor mentioned above, is that they can be difficult to book. This is especially true around holidays, eg the middle of April approaching Songkran festival, since a lot of Thais prefer the train, too. Trains out of Bangkok should be booked as far in advance as possible — a week minimum for such popular routes as the Northern (to Chieng Mai) and Southern (to Hat Yai) lines, especially if you want a sleeper. For the North-eastern and Eastern lines a few days will suffice.

Booking Trains

To book tickets in advance go to the Hualamphong station, walk through the front of the station house and go straight to the back right-hand corner where a sign says 'Advance Booking'. The other ticket windows, on the left-hand side of the station, are for same-day purchases, mostly third class. In the Advance Booking office you will receive a numbered reservation form, white for the Southern line, green for North, North-eastern, and Eastern. Then proceed into the ticketing room, taking the blank reservation form to the appropriate counter. At this point you do *not* wait for your number to be called but must fight for a place at the counter so one of the railway clerks can fill in the forms for you, according to available space on the train you want. This done, you take the filled-out form to the desk indicated by the clerk, separate your numbered stub from the form, and spindle the form on the nail standing upright on that desk. Then you must wait until your number is called (most likely in Thai, so keep an eye on the numbers around you), at which point the agent at the desk will give you your ticket and collect the money. It's not as bad as it sounds, but takes some time. Tickets between any stations in Thailand can be purchased at Hualamphong.

Ticket offices for the State Railway of Thailand are open from 8.30 am to 6 pm on weekdays, 8.30 am to 12 noon on weekends and public holidays. There is a 25B surcharge for Express trains (*rot duan*) and 15B for Rapid trains (*rot raew*). These trains are somewhat faster than the ordinary trains, as they make fewer stops. On the Northern line during the daytime there may be a 30B surcharge for air-con in second class.

The charge for second class sleeping berths is 65B for an upper berth and 95B for a lower berth. The difference is that there is a window next to the lower berth and a little more headroom. The upper berth is quite comfortable, however. No sleepers are available in third class.

Third class is not too bad, seats are harder than in second and it can be more crowded, but it costs about half as much as second class. Recommended for shorter journeys.

Train fares in Thailand recently increased quite a bit (35% for second class) so it's not quite the bargain it was. You can figure on 500 km costing about 140B in second class, twice that in first class, less than half in third. For any journey over 200 km you are allowed a stopover of two days anywhere along the route but the ticket must be endorsed by the stationmaster (fee of 1B) when you get off the train. Note that buying a return ticket does not guarantee you a seat on the way back, it only means you do not have to buy a ticket for the return. If you want a guaranteed seat reservation it's best to buy a one-way ticket for the return immediately upon arrival at your destination, not to buy a return ticket at your starting point. Kind of an odd system.

Booking trains back to Bangkok is generally not as difficult as booking trains out of Bangkok; however some stations can be quite difficult, eg buying a ticket from Surat Thani to Bangkok.

BUSES

Several different types of buses ply the roads of Thailand. Cheapest and slowest are the ordinary government-run buses. For some destinations — smaller towns — these are your only choice. The faster, more comfortable, government-run 'tour buses' (*rot tua* or *rot air*), usually with air-con, only run between certain major cities. If these are available to your destination, they are your best choice since they don't cost that much more than the ordinary stop-in-every-town buses. The government bus company is called *Baw Kaw Saw* for short.

There are different bus stations for different regions: Eastern Bus Terminal, Soi 40 Sukhumwit (tel 392-2391) for the east; Southern Bus Terminal, Charan Sanitwong Rd in Thonburi (4114978-9) for the south; Northern Bus Terminal, Phahonyothin Rd (2796621-5) for buses to the north and north-east.

Charter buses are available between Bangkok and major tourist destinations: Chieng Mai, Surat, Hat Yai, Phuket, and a few others. These are called 'tour buses' also, though there is no tour involved, and they are run by private companies. To Phuket, for example, about 10 different companies are running buses out of Bangkok every week — many of these can be booked through Bangkok hotels. Fares vary a bit from company to company, but there is usually not much difference. However, fare differences between the government and private bus companies can be substantial. Using Phuket as an example again, the state-run buses from the Southern Bus Terminal cost 134B one-way or 200B for air-con, while the privately run buses range from 220B to 280B one-way. For Chieng Mai, the private tour buses are about twice the fare of state-run buses.

There are also chartered buses running between major destinations within the various regions eg Nakhorn Si Thammarat to Hat Yai in the south, and Chieng Mai to Sukhothai in the north. New companies are cropping up all the time, there seem to be more every year, though the proliferation may be reaching its peak.

The tour buses are somewhat more comfortable than the state buses, if you don't mind narrow seats and a hair-raising ride. The trick the tour companies use to make their buses seem more comfortable is to make you think you're not on a bus, by turning up the air-con until your knees knock, handing out pillows and blankets and serving free soft drinks. On long overnight journeys the buses usually stop somewhere en route and passengers are awakened to dismount the bus for a free meal of fried rice or rice soup. One company running buses from Songkhla to Bangkok (booked through the Choke Dee Hotel) treats you to a fabulous seafood meal at Samila Beach *before* you take off for Bangkok, which is really nice.

The trouble with the tour buses is that statistically they seem to meet with a lot of accidents — head-ons with trucks, turnovers as they round a bad curve — probably because their drivers may not be as experienced on a particular route, since the companies open and fold so frequently, and because they try hard to make good time — fares are sold on a reputation for speed. Because the fares are higher than the government-run buses they attract a more well-heeled clientele among the Thais, as well as foreign tourists. One result is that a tour bus loaded with money or the promise of money has become a temptation to upcountry bandits. Hence tour buses get robbed by bands of thieves every so often, especially on the southern route between Surat & Hat Yai, and in the north between Sukhothai & Chieng Mai and Chieng Mai & Chieng Rai. The bandits lay a roadblock for the bus — almost always at night — or run the bus off the road with a truck, then board the bus and rob the passengers at gunpoint. There have also been cases of robbers riding along on the bus with concealed weapons. The Thai police patrol the dangerous areas and subject tour buses to occasional searches, so quite a few robbery attempts are thwarted. Large-scale robberies never occur on the ordinary buses, very rarely on the state-run air-con buses, and rarely on the trains, the Southern route being the most dangerous for trains. Accidents are not unknown on the state-run buses, however, so the train still comes out the safest means of transport in Thailand.

Now that you've decided not to go to Thailand after all let me point out that robberies and accidents are relatively infrequent considering the number of buses taken daily (though they are more frequent then they should be) and I've never been on a bus that's suffered either mishap — the odds are on your side. Travellers to Thailand should know the risk of tour bus travel against the apparent convenience, especially when there are alternatives. Some travellers really like the tour buses, though, so the private companies will continue to do good business.

Keep an eye on your bags when riding buses — thievery by stealth is still the most popular form of robbery in Thailand (eminently preferable to the forceful variety in my opinion), though again the risks are not that great — just be aware. The place you are most likely to be 'touched' is on the crowded buses in Bangkok. Razor artists abound, particularly on the buses in the vicinity of the Hualamphong railway station. These dexterous thieves specialize in slashing your knapsack, shoulder bag, or even your pants pockets with a sharp razor and slipping your valuables out unnoticed. Hold your bag in front of you, under your attention, and carry money in a front shirt pocket, preferably (as the Thais do), maintaining a tactile and visual sensitivity to these areas if the bus is packed shoulder to shoulder. Seasoned travellers don't need this advice as the same precautions are useful all over the world — the trick is to be relaxed but aware, not tense.

AIR TRANSPORT

Thai Airways service includes 22 cities in Thailand, plus Vientiane, Hanoi, and Penang outside the country, and it is a fairly efficient airline. Domestic fares were increased about 20% in April in 1981 so that they now are on a par with the international average.

Here are some sample fares; round-trip is double the one-way rate.

Bangkok-Chieng Mai	1100B
Bangkok-Phuket	1340B
Bangkok-Udon	750B (Avro 748)
	870B (Boeing 737-200)
Bangkok-Penang	2740B
Bangkok-Hat Yai	1530B
Bangkok-Vientiane	1500B
Chieng Mai-Mae Hong Son	280B
Khon Kaen-Phitsanuloke	470B

Flights to or within the north-east are considerably cheaper than flights to or within other regions.

CAR & MOTORCYCLE

Cars and motorcycles can be rented, outside of Bangkok, in Chieng Mai, Phuket, and Hat Yai. Check with travel agencies or large hotels for rental locations. Rental rates vary considerably from one agency to another and from city to city. Since there is a glut of motorcycles for rent in Chieng Mai these days, they can be rented there for as little as 80B per day. Motorcycles in Phuket cost up to 200B per day. A substantial deposit is usually required to rent a bike or car.

SAFETY

Several insurgent groups have been operating in Thailand for many, many years now — the Communist Party of Thailand (CPT) with its tactical force, the People's Liberation Army of Thailand (PLAT) in the north, north-east, and south, as well as the Malay separatists and Muslim revolutionaries in the south. These groups (the Thai government officially estimates about 10,000 active guerillas) are mainly involved in propaganda activity, village infiltration, and occasional clashes with Thai government troops. Very rarely have they had any encounters with foreign travellers. Aside from sporadic terrorist bombings, mostly in railway stations in the south, sometimes at up-country festivals, 'innocent' people have not been involved in the insurgent activity. The battle is between government and anti-government forces, and as long as you are not directly associated with either side there is little danger in travelling through guerilla territory.

Bangkok & Central Thailand

There is a lot to see and do in Bangkok if you can tolerate the traffic, noise, heat (in the hot season), floods (in the rainy season), and somewhat polluted air. The city is incredibly urbanized, but beneath its modern veneer lies an unmistakable Thai-ness. To say that Bangkok is not Thailand, as has been superciliously claimed by some, is like saying that New York is not America, Paris is not France, or London not England.

The capital of Thailand was established at Bangkok in 1782 by the first king of the Chakri dynasty, Rama I. The name Bangkok means 'place of olives' (not the European variety) and refers to the original site which is only a very small part of what today is called Bangkok by foreigners. The official Thai name is *Krungthepmahanakhornamonratanakosinmahaintarasiayuthayamafmapopnoppalaratehathaniprilom*, quite a tongue-twister, but is shortened to Krung Thep, 'city of angels', in everyday usage. Metropolitan Krung Thep includes Thonburi, the older part of the city (and predecessor to Bangkok as the capital), which is located across the Chao Phraya River to the west.

The east side of the river, Bangkok proper, can be divided in two by the main north-south rail line. The portion between the river and the railway is old Bangkok, where most of the older temples and the original palace is located, as well as the Chinese and Indian districts. That part of the city east of the railway, covering more than twice as much area as the old districts is 'new' Bangkok. This latter part can be divided again into the business and tourist district wedged between New Road (Charoen Krung Rd) and Rama IV Rd, and the sprawling residential and tourist district stretching out Sukhumwit and Phetburi Extension (New Phetburi) Roads. This leaves the hard-to-classify areas below Sathorn Tai Rd (which includes Klong Toey, Bangkok's main port), and the area above Rama IV Rd between the railway and Withayu Rd, which comprises an infinite variety of businesses, several movie theatres, civil service offices, the shopping area of Siam Square, Chulalongkorn University, and the National Stadium.

Getting around in Bangkok may be difficult at first for the uninitiated but once you've got the bus system down the whole city is accessible. Bangkok was once called the Venice of the East, but the canal system is fast disappearing to give way to more road construction — with 10% of Thailand's population living in the capital, water transportation, with few exceptions, is a thing of the past. Those canals that do remain are hopelessly polluted and will probably be filled in by the end of the century.

Bangkok caters to diverse interests: there are temples, museums, and other historic sites for those interested in traditional Thai culture, and an endless variety of good restaurants, clubs, international cultural and social events, movies in several different languages, and a modern art institute, for those seeking contemporary Krung Thep.

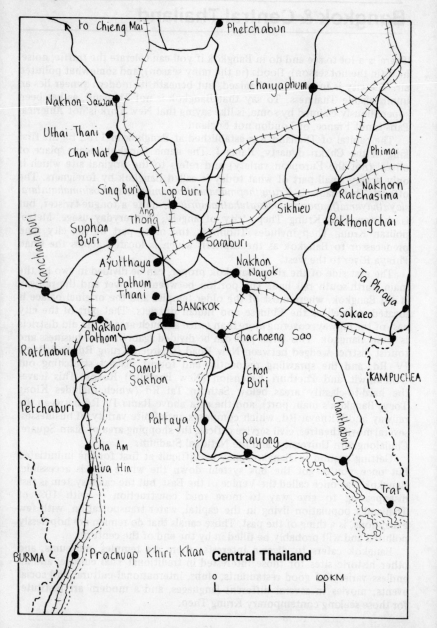

to Chieng Mai

Phetchabun

Chaiyaphum

Nakhon Sawan

Uthai Thani

Chai Nat

Phimai

Sing Buri

Lop Buri

Ang Thong

Sikhieu

Nakhorn Ratchasima

Pakthongchai

Suphan Buri

Saraburi

Kanchanaburi

Ayutthaya

Nakhon Nayok

Ta Phraya

Pathum Thani

BANGKOK

Sakaeo

Nakhon Pathom

Chachoeng Sao

Ratchaburi

Samut Sakhon

Chon Buri

KAMPUCHEA

Petchaburi

Pattaya

Chanthaburi

Cha Am

Rayong

Hua Hin

Trat

BURMA

Prachuap Khiri Khan

Central Thailand

0   100 KM

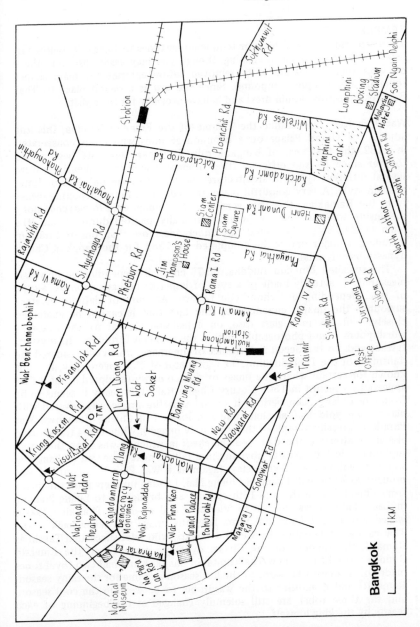

Bangkok

1KM

TEMPLES

There are close to 400 *wats* or temple-monasteries in Bangkok. Below are listed some of the most interesting, though you may easily discover others on your own. Shoes are to be removed before entering the main chapel (*bot*) in any temple compound. Since the *wat* is a sacred place to Thai Buddhists, visitors should dress and behave decently for their visit.

Wat Phra Keo Also called the Temple of the Emerald Buddha, this *wat* adjoins the Grand Palace on a common grounds which was consecrated in 1782, the first year of Bangkok rule. Together they have been added to ever since by the different Thai monarchs and consequently feature several different types of architecture, most of it in the Bangkok or Ratanakosin style. A very colourful place, the *wat* has a mural depicting scenes from the Ramakien, the Thai version of the Indian epic *Ramayana*, along the inside walls of the compound. Originally painted during Rama III's reign (1824-1850), the mural has undergone more than one restoration, including a major one to be completed by 1982 for the Bangkok/Chakri dynasty bicentennial.

The so-called Emerald Buddha, 60-75 cm high (depending on how it is measured), is actually made of a type of jasper or perhaps nephrite, a type of jade, depending on whom you believe. An aura of definite mystery surrounds the image, enhanced by the fact that it cannot be examined closely — it sits in a glass case, on a pedestal high above the heads of worshippers — and photography within the chapel is forbidden. Its mystery further adds to the occult significance of the image, which is considered the 'talisman' of the Thai kingdom, the legitimator of Thai sovereignty. It is not known for certain where the image originated or who sculpted it but it first appeared on record in 15th century Chieng Rai; stylistically it seems to be from the Chieng Saen period. It is said that the image was covered with plaster and gold leaf at that time and located in Chieng Rai's own Wat Phra Keo (literally 'temple of the jewel holy image'). While being transported elsewhere after a storm damaged the *chedi* in which it was kept, the image supposedly lost its plaster covering in a fall. It next appeared in Lampang where it enjoyed a 32-year stay (again at a Wat Phra Keo) until it was brought to Wat Chedi Luang in Chieng Mai. Laotian invaders took the image from Chieng Mai in the mid-16th century and brought it to Luang Prabang in Laos. Later it was moved to Vientiane and when the Thai king Taksin waged war against Laos 200 years later the image was taken back to the Thai capital of Thonburi by General Chakri, who later succeeded Taksin as Rama I, the founder of the Chakri dynasty. Rama I had the Emerald Buddha moved to the new Thai capital in Bangkok and had two royal robes made for it, one to be worn in the hot season and one for the rainy season. Rama III added another to the wardrobe, to be worn in the cool season, and the three robes are still solemnly changed at the beginning of each season by the king himself.

The palace itself is only used by the king on certain ceremonial occasions (eg Coronation Day), as his residence is now Chitlada Palace in the northern part of the city. The Grand Palace was the headquarters for the attempted coup by General San Chitpatima in April 1981.

Admission to Wat Phra Keo is free on Sundays and public holidays, and 15B on all other days. Hours are 8.30 am to noon and 1-4 pm.

Wat Mahathat A very old monastery, Wat Mahathat is worth a visit as it is right across the street from Wat Phra Keo, on the west side of Sanam Luang. This *wat* is a national centre for the Mahanikai monastic sect and houses one of Bangkok's two Buddhist universities. Check out the pigeons in the courtyard behind the main temple.

No admission charge.

Wat Pho (Wat Phra Jetuphon) A long list of superlatives for this one: the oldest and largest *wat* in Bangkok, it features the largest reclining Buddha and the largest collection of Buddha images in Thailand, and was the earliest centre for public education. As a temple site Wat Pho dates back supposedly to the 16th century but its current history really begins in 1781 with the renovation of the original monastery. Narrow Jetuphon Rd divides the grounds in two; each portion is surrounded by huge whitewashed walls but the most interesting portion is the northern compound, which includes a very large *bot* enclosed by a gallery of Buddha images and four *wiharns*, four large *chedis*, commemorating the first four Chakri kings, 91 smaller *chedis*, an old *tripitaka* library, a sermon-hall, the large *wiharn* which houses the reclining Buddha, and a school building for classes in *abhidhamma* (Buddhist philosophy), plus several less important structures. A massage school of sorts convenes in the afternoons at the west end of the compound.

The tremendous reclining Buddha, 46 metres long and 15 metres high, illustrates the passing of the Buddha into final Nirvana. The figure is modelled of plaster around a brick core, and finished in gold leaf. Mother-of-pearl inlay ornaments the eyes and feet of the colossal image, the feet displaying 108 different auspicious *laksanas* or characteristics of a Buddha. The images on display in the four *wiharns* surrounding the main *bot* in the east part of the compound are interesting, particularly the Phra Jinaraj and Phra Jinachi Buddhas, located in the west and south chapels, both from Sukhothai. The galleries extending between the four chapels feature no less than 394 gilded Buddha images.

The temple rubbings for sale at Wat Pho and elsewhere in Thailand come from the reliefs sculpted in the base of the large *bot*, which are carved in marble and were obtained from the ruins of Ayuthaya. The rubbings are no longer taken directly from the panels but are rubbed from cement casts of the panels made years ago.

Wat Traimit The 'Temple of the Golden Buddha' is situated where Yaowarat

Rd and Charoen Krung Rd intersect, near the Hualamphong Railway Station. The attraction at this old *wat* is, of course, the impressive three-metre tall, 5½-tonne solid gold Buddha image, which gleams like no other gold artifact I've ever seen. Sculpted in the graceful Sukhothai style, the image was 'rediscovered' some 30 years ago beneath a stucco or plaster exterior when it fell from a crane while being moved to a new building within the temple compound. It has been theorized that the covering was added to protect it from 'marauding hordes' either during the late Sukhothai period or later in Ayuthaya when the city was under seige by the Burmese. The temple itself is said to date to the early 13th century.

Admission to Wat Traimit is free.

Wat Arun The 'Temple of Dawn' is named for the Indian god of the dawn, Aruna. It appears in all the tourist brochures and is located on the Thonburi side of the Chao Phraya River. The tall, 82-metre *prang* was constructed during the first half of the 19th century by Rama II and Rama III, and is composed of a brick core with a plaster covering imbedded with a mosaic of broken Chinese porcelain. The present *wat* is built on the site of Wat Chang, which was the palace and royal temple of King Taksin when Thonburi was the Thai capital; hence, it was the last home of the Emerald Buddha before Rama I brought it across the river to Bangkok.

The place looks more impressive from the river than it does up close, though the peaceful *wat* grounds make a very nice retreat from the hustle-bustle of Bangkok. The main tower can be climbed by means of steep stairs to over half its height and provides a fine view of Thonburi and the river.

To reach Wat Arun from the Bangkok side catch a river taxi going down-river from the pier at Na Phra Lan Rd (near Wat Phra Keo) or the one at Thai Wang Rd (near Wat Pho), and it will stop at the Wat Arun landing.

Wat Arun is open daily; the admission fee is 5B.

Wat Benchamabophit — Si Ayuthaya and Rama V Rds. Built at the turn of the century under Chulalongkorn (Rama V) of white Carrara marble, the large *bot* at Wat Ben is a prime example of modern Thai architecture. The courtyard behind the *bot* exhibits 53 Buddha images, most of which are copies of famous images/styles from throughout Thailand and other Buddhist countries, an education in itself if you're interested in Buddhist iconography.

Admission is free and the *wat* is open daily.

Wat Saket Saket is an undistinguished temple except for the Golden Mount (Phu Khao Thong) on the west side of the grounds which provides a good view of Bangkok rooftops. The artificial hill was created when a large *chedi* under construction by Rama III collapsed because the soft soil beneath would not support it. The resulting mud-and-brick hill was left to sprout weeds until Rama IV built a small *chedi* on its crest. Later his son, Rama V, added to the structure and housed a Buddha relic from India (given to him by the British government) in the *chedi*. The concrete walls were added during WW II, to prevent the hill from eroding. Every November there is a big festival on the grounds of Wat Saket, which includes a candle-lit procession up the Golden Mount.

Admission to Wat Saket is free except for the final approach to the summit of the Golden Mount, which costs 1B.

Wat Rajanadda — across Mahachai Rd from Wat Saket, behind the Chalerm Thai movie theatre. This temple dates to the mid-19th century, build under Rama III, and is an unusual specimen, possibly influenced by Burmese models. There is a well-known amulet market here selling all sizes, shapes, and styles of Buddhist amulets or magic charms, (called *phra phim* in Thai) which feature not only images of the Buddha but famous Thai monks and Indian deities. This is an expensive place to purchase a charm, but a good place to look; these images are purported to protect the wearer from physical harm usually, though some act as 'love charms'. Those amulets that are considered to be particularly powerful cost thousands of baht, and are worn by soldiers, taxi drivers, and other Thai believers working in high-risk professions.

Wat Bowonniwet (Bowornives) — Phra Sumen Rd. Wat Bowon is the national headquarters for the Thammayut monastic sect, the minority sect in relation to Mahanikai. King Mongkut, founder of the Thammayuts, began a royal traditional by residing here as a monk — in fact he was the abbot of Wat Bowon for several years. Bangkok's second Buddhist university, Mahamakut University, is housed here and there is an excellent English-language Buddhist bookstore across the street from the main entrance to the wat.

OTHER ATTRACTIONS
National Museum — Na Phrathat Rd, west side of Sanam Luang.
Said to be the largest museum in South-East Asia, this is an excellent place to learn something about Thai art before heading upcountry. All periods and styles are represented, from Dvaravati to Ratanakosin, and English-language literature is available. Free English tours of the museum are given on Tuesdays (Thai culture), Wednesdays (Buddhism) and Thursdays (Thai art), beginning at 9.30 am. The museum is open 9 am to noon and 1-4 pm every day except Monday and Friday; admission is free on weekends but 5B on weekdays.

National Theatre — Na Phrathat and Chao Fa Rds.
Check with the National Theatre if you are interested in Thai classical drama, *lakhorn*. Performances are usually excellent and admission fees very

reasonable, around 30B depending on the seating. Attendance at a *khon* performance (masked dance-drama based on stories from the Ramakien) is highly recommended.

Lak Muang ('City Pillar') **Shrine** — Across the street from the east wall of Wat Phra Keo, at the south end of Sanam Luang.

This shrine encloses a wooden pillar erected by Rama I to represent the founding of the new Bangkok capital. The spirit of the pillar is considered the city's guardian deity and receives the daily supplications of countless Thai worshippers, some of whom commission classical Thai dancers to perform at the shrine.

Jim Thompson's House — Soi Kasem San 2, Rama I Rd.

This is a great place to visit, even though it sounds hokey when described, for its authentic Thai residential architecture. Located at the end of an undistinguished Bangkok *soi* next to Khlong San Saep, the premises once belonged to the American silk entrepreneur Jim Thompson, who deserves most of the credit for the current worldwide popularity of Thai silk. Thompson disappeared in the Cameron Highlands of west Malaysia under quite mysterious circumstances in 1967, and has never been heard from since. On display in the main house is his splendid little Asian art collection as well as his personal belongings.

An excellent book on Thompson, his career, residence, and intriguing disappearance is available: *The Legendary American — The Remarkable Career and Strange Disappearance of Jim Thompson* by William Warren (Boston: Houghton Mifflin Co 1970).

The house is only open Monday and Thursday mornings, admission is 30B (proceeds go to Bangkok's School for the Blind) but you may wander around the grounds for free. The rather sleazy *khlong* at the end of the *soi* is one of Bangkok's most lively.

Chinatown (Sampeng) — off Yaowarat and Ratchawong Rds.

Bangkok's Chinatown comprises a confusing and crowded array of jewellery, hardware, wholesale food, automotive, and fabric shops, as well as dozens of other small businesses. It's a good place to shop since goods here are cheaper than almost anywhere else in Bangkok, and the Chinese proprietors like to bargain. Chinese and Thai antiques in various grades of age and authenticity are available in the so-called Thieves' Market or Nakhorn Kasem, better for browsing than buying these days.

At the edge of Chinatown around the intersection of Pahurath and Chakraphet Rds is a small but thriving Indian district, generally called *Pahurath*. Here are located dozens of Indian-owned shops selling all kinds of fabric/clothes, and this is the best place in the city to bargain for such items, especially silk. The selection is unbelievable. Thai shoulder bags (*yahms*) here are the cheapest in Bangkok, perhaps in Thailand. Behind the more obvious store fronts along these streets, in the 'bowels' of the blocks, is a seemingly endless Indian bazaar selling not only fabric, but household items, food and other necessities. There are some good, reasonably priced Indian restaurants in this area, too, and a Sikh temple off Chakraphet Rd.

Thai Boxing

Muay Thai, or Thai boxing, can be seen at two boxing stadiums, Lumpini (on Rama IV Rd near South Sathorn Rd) and Ratchadamnoen (on Ratchadamnoen Nok Rd, next to the TAT office). Admission fees vary according to seating — cheapest in Bangkok is 25B; Monday, Wednesday, Thursday, and Sunday the boxing is at Ratchadamnoen and Tuesday, Wednesday, Friday, and Saturday it is at Lumpini.

Almost anything goes in this martial sport, both in the ring and in the stands. If you don't mind the violence (in the ring) a Thai boxing match is worth attending for the pure spectacle — the wild musical accompaniment, the ceremonial beginning of each match, the frenzied betting around the stadium. The restaurant next to the Ratchadamnoen Stadium is well-known for its esteemed *kai yang*.

Thai Classical Dancing

If you are not able to catch a free performance at the Lak Muang or Erawan Hotel shrines or one at the National Theatre, there are several restaurants and hotels that specialize in performances for tourists. Admission charges range from 140B-180B and include a sumptuous Thai meal as well as martial art and sword-fighting demonstrations. One of the better places is the Baan Thai on Soi 32 (Soi Baan Thai) Sukhumwit Rd — the food is very good and is served in a traditional manner with diners seated at low tables. If you're looking for a splurge this might be it.

The historic Oriental Hotel on Charoen Krung Rd offers free dance/ martial art performances in the riverside garden every Sunday and Thursday at 11 am.

Floating Markets and Canal Tours

Travellers who have been to the Thonburi floating market on Khlong Dao Kanong in recent years are divided as to whether the trip is worth the early rising to get there by 7-7.30 am. There are still plenty of boats out there, selling fresh produce and ready-to-eat foods, but there may be as many boatloads of tourists, too. If you're set on going it might be best to take one of the floating market tours that leave from the Oriental pier (Soi Oriental) or Tha Phra Chan beside Thammasat University — your only alternative is to hire a boat of your own (at the Oriental pier) to go up Khlong Dao Kanong and that·can be quite expensive these days. Khlong Dao Kanong is located in south Thonburi, across the river from the terminus of Charoen Krung Rd, below Krung Thep Bridge.

There is a much more lively and less touristed floating market on Khlong

Damnoen Saduak in Rajburi province, 104 km south-west of Bangkok, between Nakhorn Pathom and Samut Songkhram. Unless you take a tour or rent a car, it could be difficult to get to; if you are determined, spend the night in Nakhorn Pathom and catch an early morning bus out of Nakhorn Pathom headed for Samut Songkhram, asking to be let out at Damnoen Saduak.

For 10B you can take a Chao Phraya River Taxi from Thanon Tok (end of Charoen Krung Rd and terminus for bus Nos. 1 and 22) as far north as Nonburi, a nice three-hour trip with lots to see along the way. Another good boat trip is the Bangkok Noi canal taxi route which leaves from Tha Phra Chan next to Thammasat University. The fare is only a few baht and the farther up Khlong Bangkok Noi you go, the better the scenery gets — teak houses on stilts, old *wats*, plenty of greenery — as if you were upcountry, and, in a sense, you are.

Weekend Market — Sanam Luang or Phra Men grounds.
The Disneyland of markets, everything is sold here, from live chickens and snakes to opium pipes and herbal remedies. Traditional Thai clothing such as the *phaakhama* (wraparound for men) and the *phaasin* (same for women), and the *maw hawm* (blue cotton farmer's shirt) are good buys, household goods like pots and pans, too, if you're moving to Thailand for an extended period. Plenty of interesting food is on sale for hungry shoppers. Don't forget to bargain.

The market is in operation all day Saturday and Sunday. Highly recommended.

Snake Farm — at the Pasteur Institute, Rama IV Rd.
Here venomous snakes are milked daily at 11 am to make snake bite antidotes which are distributed throughout the country. Boring to some, exciting to others.

Admission is 10B.

Siam Society — Soi 21 Sukhumwit Rd.
Publishers of the renowned *Journal of the Siam Society* and valiant preservers of traditional Thai culture. The Society headquarters is a good place to visit for those with a serious interest in Thailand — a reference library is open to visitors and Siam Society monographs are for sale. Almost anything you'd want to know about Thailand (outside the political sphere, since the Society is sponsored by the royal family) can be researched here. An ethnological museum of sorts, exhibiting Thai folk art, is located on the Siam Society grounds in the Kamthieng House.

NIGHTLIFE
Bangkok is loaded with coffeeshops, nightclubs, and massage parlours, many of them left over from the days when the City of Angels was an R&R

stop for GI's serving in Viet Nam. By and large they are seedy, expensive, and cater to men only. All the major hotels have flashy nightclubs, too, less seedy but more expensive. Many feature live music — rock, country & western, Thai pop music, and jazz, the latter usually played by good Filipino bands.

The girlie bars are concentrated along Sukhumwit Rd from Soi 21 on out; off Sukhumwit on Soi Nana (including the infamous Grace Hotel); and on Phat Phong Rds I & II, between Silom and Suriwong Rds. Most are pretty tame nowadays, at least in terms of the excitement you get for your money, though Soi Cowboy (off Sukhumwit) still gets pretty wild some nights.

Massage parlours have been a Bangkok attraction for many years now, though the Tourist Authority of Thailand tries to discourage the city's reputation in this respect. Massage as a healing art is a tradition that is centuries old in Thailand (check out Wat Pho) and it is still possible to get a really legitimate massage in Bangkok — this despite the commercialization of recent years. That many of the massage parlours also deal in prostitution is well-known; less well-known is the fact that many (but by no means all) of the girls working in the parlours are bonded labour — they are not there by choice. It takes a pretty sexist male not to be saddened by the sight of 50 girls/women behind a glass wall with numbers pinned to their dresses. Should male travellers avail themselves of more than a massage and come down with something they hadn't bargained for, there are plenty of VD clinics located along Ploenchit Rd.

For more high-brow entertainment, there is the Alliance Francaise, next to the YMCA on Sathorn Tai Rd, which shows several French films each week. Showtimes are usually 8 pm (titles and show-times are posted outside the main building) and admission is 20B for members, 30B for non-members. There are also a dozen or more Thai movie theatres around town showing Thai, Chinese, Indian, and occasional Western (European and American) movies. These theatres are air-conditioned and quite comfortable, with reasonable rates. All movies in Thai theatres are preceded by the Thai national anthem along with pictures of King Bhumiphol and other members of the royal family projected on the screen. Everyone in the theatre stands quietly for the duration of the anthem (written by the king, incidently) in respect for the monarch. Films are listed in the daily *Bangkok Post* newspaper — look for other cultural events in the paper, too, there are occasional classical music performances, rock concerts, Asian music/theatre ensembles on tour, art shows, international buffets, etc. Boredom should not be a problem in Bangkok, at least not for a short-term visit; however, save some money for your upcountry trip!

OUTSIDE BANGKOK

AYUTHAYA

Approximately 86 km north of Bangkok, this city was the Thai capital from 1350 to 1767 and was a splendid city by all accounts. Prior to 1350, when the capital was moved here from U Thong, it was a Khmer outpost.

Thirty-three kings of various Siamese dynasties reigned in Ayuthaya until it was conquered by the Burmese. During its heyday, Thai culture and international commerce flourished in the kingdom — the Ayuthaya period has so far been the apex of Thai history — and Ayuthaya was courted by Dutch, Portuguese, French, English, Chinese, and Japanese merchants. All comers claimed it to be the most illustrious city they had ever seen.

The present-day city is located at the confluence of three rivers, the Chao Phraya, the Pa Sak, and the smaller Lopburi. A wide canal joins them and makes a complete circle around the town. Long-tail boats can be rented from the boat landing across from Chandra Kasem (Chan Kasem) Palace for a tour around the river/canal; several of the old *wat* ruins (Wat Phanam Choeng, Wat Phuttaisawan, Wat Kasatrathira, and Wat Chai Wattanaram) may be glimpsed in this way, as well as picturesque river life. Outside of the historic ruins and museums, Ayuthaya is not particularly interesting but it is one of three cities in Thailand known for their 'gangster' activity.

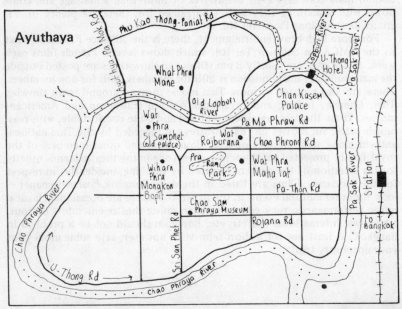

Things to See
National Museum There are two. The main one is called the Chao Sam Phraya Museum, and is near the intersection of Rojana Rd (Ayuthaya's main street, connecting with the highway to Bangkok) and Si Sanphet Rd, opposite the city hall near the centre of town. It is open 9 am-4 pm Wednesday through Sunday, with a 2B admission fee. The second, Chan Kasem Palace (*Phra Ratchawong Chan Kasem*), is a museum piece itself, built by the 17th king of Ayuthaya — Maha Thammaraj — for his son Prince Naresuan. It is in the Chan Kasem Palace in the north-east corner of the town, near the river. Hours are the same there as at the other museum. Pick up a good map/guide of Ayuthaya at the museum for 15B.

Wat Phra Si Sanphet
This was the largest temple in Ayuthaya in its time, used as the Royal Temple-Palace for several Ayuthaya kings. Built in the 14th century, the compound once contained a 16-metre standing Buddha covered with 250 kg of gold, which was melted down by the Burmese conquerors. It is mainly known for the *chedis* erected in the quintessential Ayuthaya style, which has come to be identified with Thai art more than any other single style.

Wiharn Phra Mongkon Bopit
Near Si Sanphet, this monastery contains one of Thailand's largest Buddha images. The present *wiharn* was built in 1956.

Wat Phra Maha That
This *wat*, located at the corner of Chee Kun and Naresuan Rds, dates to the 14th century, but not much was left standing by the Burmese hordes. Despite extensive ruin, the *prang* is still impressive.

Wat Rajburana
Counterpart ruins to Maha That across the road; the *chedis* are not quite as dilapidated, however.

Wat Phra Chao Phanam Choeng
This one was built before Ayuthaya became a Siamese capital, located right on the Chao Phraya River outside the town proper to the south-east. The main *wiharn* contains a highly revered 19-metre sitting Buddha image.

Wat Na Phra Mane (Phra Meru)
Across from the old Royal Palace (*wang luang*) grounds is a bridge which can be crossed to arrive at Wat Phra Mane. This temple is notable because it escaped destruction in 1767, though it has required restoration over the years anyway. Recommended.

Wat Thammik Raj
To the west of the old palace grounds, inside the river loop, Thammik Raj features overgrown *chedi* ruins and lion sculptures.

Wat Yai Chai Mongkon
Wat Yai, as the locals call it, lies outside the city to the south-east a way but can be reached by minibus for 3-4B. It's a quiet old place that was once a famous meditation *wat*, built in 1357 by King U Thong. The compound contains a very large *chedi* from which the *wat* takes its popular name (*yai* = big), and there is a community of *mae chee* or Buddhist nuns (actually laywomen since the Sangha does not officially admit women into the order) residing here.

Getting to Ayuthaya
Ayuthaya can be reached by bus, train, or boat. Daily buses leave from the Northern Bus Terminal in Bangkok every 10 minutes, 5 am-7 pm, the fare is 14B and the trip takes 1½ hours. Trains leave from the Hualamphong railway station at 4.45 am, 5.50 am, 6.30 am, 7.20 am, 8.10 am, 9 am, 9.30 am, 10.40 am, 11.45 am, 12.25 pm, 1 pm, 2.20 pm, 3.30 pm, 4.05 pm, 4.30 pm, 4.45 pm, 5.20 pm, and 6.10 pm; third class fare is 14B for the 1½-hour trip.

Boats to Ayuthaya leave Bangkok from Tha Thien pier near Thammasat daily at about 10 am but the trip is rather long going upriver. Better to take the boat back from Ayuthaya — about three hours or so. Check at the landing near Chan Kasem Palace in Ayuthaya for the current fare and departure time.

BANG PA IN
20 km south of Ayuthaya. A rather rococco palace surrounded by a lake is the attraction here, not particularly noteworthy, but a nice boat trip from Ayuthaya. Can be reached by minibus from Ayuthaya's Chao Phom market, Chao Phom Rd, for 6B.

LOPBURI
154 km north of Bangkok. Called Lavo during the Dvaravati period, this settlement was inhabited at least as far back as the sixth century. The partially ruined Kala shrine in the town's centre is all the architecture that remains from the pre-Khmer period. The Khmers took over Lavo in the 11th century and so most of the old *wats* here feature Khmer architecture.

Noteworthy sites in Lopburi
Prang Khaek   A Hindu temple with three *prangs* (Khmer-style super-structures) from the 11th century.

Phra Prang Sam Yod   This one has three *prangs*, too, but is considered by art historians to be the finest specimen of Khmer architecture in the area. The dating is as yet uncertain for this monument but it is probably late 12th or early 13th century.

Phaulkon's House Walk towards the river from Prang Khaek to find this one across the street. Former home of the infamous Greek, the building is very European in ambience.

Getting to Lopburi

Buses leave for Lopburi every 10 minutes from Ayuthaya, or, if you're coming from Bangkok, about every 20 minutes (5.21 am to 8.29 pm) from the Northern Terminal, 26B and a three-hour ride.

An Express train leaves Hualamphong station daily for Lopburi (and beyond) at 6 pm, arriving in Lopburi at 8.20 pm; a Rapid train leaves at 3 pm, arriving at 5.24 pm; ordinary trains leave at 9.30 am and 8 pm, arriving at 12.30 pm and 10.47 pm respectively. Train fare is 49B second class, 26B third.

WEST OF BANGKOK

NAKHORN PATHOM

56 km from Bangkok. Regarded as the oldest city in Thailand, Nakhorn Pathom was the centre of the Dvaravati kingdom, a loose collection of city states that flourished between the sixth and 11th centuries AD in the Chao Phraya River valley. The area has probably been inhabited at least since India's Ashokan period (third century BC), as it is theorized that Buddhist missionaries from India visited Nakhorn Pathom at that time.

The central attraction here is the famous Phra Pathom Chedi, the single tallest Buddhist monument in the world, rising to 127 metres. The original monument, buried within the massive orange-glazed dome, was erected in the early sixth century by the Theravada Buddhists of Dvaravati, but in the early 11th century the Khmer King Suryavarman I of Angkor conquered the city and built a Brahman *prang* over the sanctuary. The Pagan Burmese, under King Anuruddha, sacked the city in 1057 and it was in ruins until King Mongkut had it restored in 1860, building a larger *chedi* over the remains according to Buddhist tradition, adding four *wiharns*, a *bot*, a replica of the original *chedi* and assorted *salas, prangs*, and other embellishments.

On the east side of the monument, in the *bot*, is a Dvaravati style Buddha seated in 'European pose', that is, in a chair, similar to the one in Wat Phra Men in Ayuthaya. It may, in fact, have come from Phra Men.

A museum is opposite the *bot*, open Wednesday through Sunday from 9 am to noon and 1-4 pm, and it contains some Dvaravati sculpture of interest.

Beside the *chedi*, the other foci of the city are Silpakorn University, west of the *chedi* off Phetkasem Highway, and Sanam Chan, adjacent to the University. Sanam Chan is a pleasant park with a canal passing through it, formerly the grounds for Rama VI's palace. The somewhat rundown palace still stands in the park but entrance is not permitted.

Getting to Nakhorn Pathom
Buses for Nakhorn Pathom leave the Southern Bus Terminal in Bangkok every 10 minutes from 6.30 am to 8.20 pm, fare is 10B for the one-hour trip. Trains leave the Bangkok Noi railway station daily at 8 am, arriving in Nakhorn Pathom at 9.08. Third class fare, recommended for such a short distance, is 13B.

KANCHANABURI
130 km west of Bangkok. Located in a slightly elevated valley of the Mae Klang River amidst hills and sugar cane plantations, Kanchanaburi was originally established by Rama I as a first line of defence against the Burmese who might use the old invasion route through Three Pagodas Pass on the Thai-Burmese border. During WW II the Japanese occupation in Thailand used Allied prisoners of war to build the infamous Death Railway along this same invasion route, in reverse, along the Kwae Noi River to the Pass. Thousands and thousands of prisoners died as a result of brutal treatment by their captors, a story chronicled by Boulle's book *The Bridge Over the River Kwai* and popularized by a movie based on the same. The bridge is still there to be seen (still in use, in fact) and so are the graves of the Allied soldiers — but the river is spelled and pronounced Khwae, like 'quack' without the '-ck'.

The medium-sized town of Kanchanaburi also offers one of the only established indoor *likhee* theatres in the country. *Likhee* is a bawdy Thai folk drama of sorts, given to comic improvisation and all-night performances — highly recommended entertainment. The *likhee* theatre in Kanchanaburi is located in a movie theatre whose construction was never quite finished, just off the main highway from Bangkok near the town entrance. The town itself has a charming atmosphere.

Getting to Kanchanaburi
The State Railway of Thailand offers a 'special diesel railcar' trip to Kanchanaburi every weekend and holiday, stopping in Nakhorn Pathom for a short tour, then on to the Khwae River bridge and beyond to Nam Tok, the end of the line, where you can take a minibus for a few baht to Khao Pang waterfall. The train leaves at 6.30 am from Hualamphong station in Bangkok, returning to Bangkok at 7.30 pm. Round trip fare for this excursion is 45B.

Buses leave the Southern Bus Terminal on the hour, 20B for the 1½ hour ride, one-way. Ordinary trains for Kanchanaburi and the River Khwae

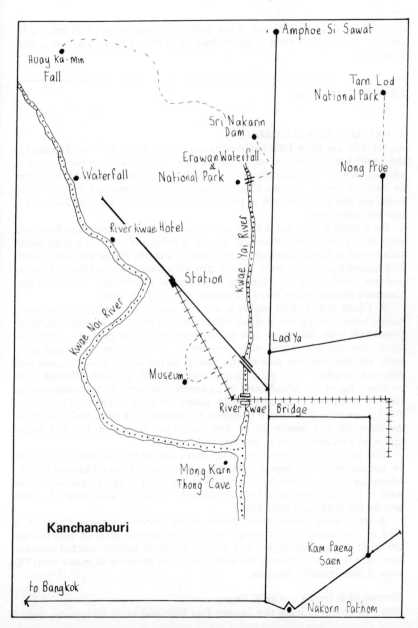

Bridge leave daily at 6.05 am, 8 am, and 2 pm, arriving at 11.21 am, 10.28 am (the number 171 train is faster than the 349), and 2.40 pm; fare is 26B third class.

EAST OF BANGKOK

SI RACHA — KOH SI CHANG

About 105 km from Bangkok on the east coast of the Gulf of Thailand is the small town of Si Racha, home of spicy Si Racha sauce (*nam phrik si rachaa*). Some of Thailand's best seafood, accompanied by this sauce, can be had here, especially the local oysters. The motor *samlors* in this fishing town are unlike those seen anywhere else — more like motorcycles with a side-car in the rear.

On a small rocky island (Koh Loi) connected to the mainland by a long jetty is a Thai-Chinese Buddhist temple. Farther off shore is a large island called Koh Si Chang flanked by two smaller islands, Kham Yai to the north and Khang Kao to the south. These provide a natural shelter from the wind and sea, used by large incoming freighters as a harbour — smaller boats transport goods to the Chao Phraya delta some 50 km away.

Si Chang island itself makes a nifty getaway. The island is practically uninhabited except for a small village on the coast facing the mainland, populated with fishermen and other mariners, and a monastic hermitage along the island's centre ridge, ensconced in limestone caves and palm huts. On the opposite side of the island, facing out to sea, are some nice deserted beaches with good snorkeling — watch the tide, though. The northern tip of the island has a good beach area, also. At the south-eastern end of Si Chang is an abandoned palace of King Chulalongkorn, never finished because the French occupied the island for a brief period in 1893. As there do not appear to be any hotels on the island, this old palace makes an excellent place to pass the night, *gratuit*.

The hermit caves along the ridge make an interesting visit, but should be approached with respect — monks come from all over Thailand to take advantage of the peaceful environment for their religious practices. This area is co-inhabited by a tribe of friendly monkeys who make the trees around the hermitage their home.

A tasty snack called *mieng kham*, rarely found so close to Bangkok, is sold in the streets of the village. Wrapped in a fresh betel or wild tea leaf are small pieces of garlic, hot pepper, dried shrimp, peanut, toasted coconut, lime, and a sweet-salty-sour tamarind sauce, to be eaten all in one bite. The taste is indescribably pleasant.

Getting to Si Racha — Koh Si Chang

Buses to Si Racha leave the Eastern Bus Terminal every 25 minutes from 5 am to 6.50 pm. The trip is 100 minutes, fare is 19B.

Koh Si Chang can be reached by boarding a ferry that leaves each morning around 8 am. The fare varies according to whose boat is making the trip. Boats can be hired for around 200B from the local mariners if you can't make the ferry boat. Either way the trip takes about an hour.

PATTAYA

On the road through Pattaya city, before Pattaya Beach, the bus passes no less than 5 prosperous sign-making businesses. Arriving at Pattaya Beach, the reason for their prosperity is immediately apparent — the place is lit up like Hollywood Boulevard at night. Most non-tourists will find Pattaya lacking in good taste as well as culture and would do well to preclude it from their itineraries. Pattaya Beach is not much of a beach to begin with, and its biggest businesses, water sports and street sex, have driven prices for food and accommodation beyond Bangkok level.

A great place for a sailor on leave, I suppose — Pattaya, in fact, got its start as a resort when there was an American base at nearby Sattaheep — since there are plenty of sailors about, both Thai and American. Food is good here, as claimed, but way over-priced. Lately that part of South Pattaya known as 'the village' has attracted a large number of *ka-toeys*, Thai transvestites, posing as hookers who ply their trade among the droves of well-heeled European tourists.

There are four or five nice islands off Pattaya's shore, expensive to get to, but if you're a snorkeling or scuba enthusiast equipment can be booked at any of the several diving shops/schools at Pattaya Beach. Koh Laan, the most popular of the offshore islands, even has places to stay.

RAYONG

Good swimming at the fairly secluded beaches here. Rayong province produces fine fruit (pineapple, durian) and *nam pla* (fish sauce). Since there is very little in the way of 'concessions' for the foreign visitor, Rayong attracts the adventurous traveller; if you're one of them, check it out, this is a *real* Thai beach.

EATING & SLEEPING IN CENTRAL THAILAND

BANGKOK

There is really quite a variety of places to stay in Bangkok, only some are harder to find than others. Your choice actually depends on what part of the city you want to be located in — the tourist ghetto of Sukhumwit Rd, the 'world traveller' ghetto of Soi Ngam Duphli around the Malaysia Hotel off Rama IV, the Siam Square area, Chinatown, or Banglamphu (north of Ratchadamnoen Klang). Chinatown/Hualamphong and Banglamphu are the

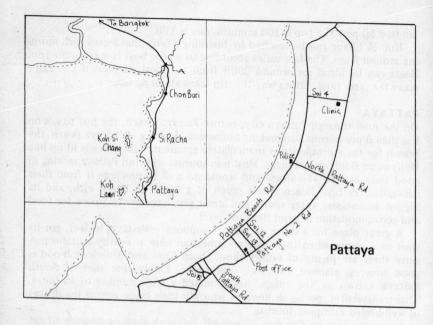

Pattaya

best all-round areas for seeing the real Bangkok and are the cheapest districts for eating and sleeping. The Siam Square area is well-located, too, in that it's more or less in the centre of Bangkok — this, coupled with the good selection of city buses that pass through the Rama I-Phayathai Rd intersection, makes even more of the city accessible. In addition, Siam Square has a good bookstore, several banks, cheap foodstalls and excellent middle-priced restaurants, travel agencies, and three movie theatres. Don't confuse Siam Square with the Siam Centre across the street, a monstrous air-conditioned shopping complex for foreigners and rich Thais.

A Foot bridge over the Ping River, Chieng Mai
B Phra Pathom Chedi, Nakhorn Pathom
C Monk at Wat Hueng Mang, Chieng Mai

Soi Ngam Duphli This area, off Rama IV Rd, where the Malaysia, Boston Inn, and Privacy Hotels are located, is where most budget travellers come on their first trip to Bangkok. These places are not particularly cheap and are sometimes full but the area is easy to deal with for first-timers since just about everyone speaks English. The entrance to this *soi* is on Rama IV Rd, near the intersection with Sathorn Tai Rd, within walking distance of the imposing Dusit Thani Hotel and Lumphini Park.

Malaysia — 54 Ngam Duphli. 120 air-con rooms, 172B for a double, including tax; a single goes for 167B. Crowded usually, the Malaysia has an interesting notice board — but don't believe everything you read, some genuine misinformation is posted there along with the good stuff. Rooms are over-priced for their condition and some thievery has been reported.

Privacy Also air-con only, 160B for a double. Many 'short-time' residents here give the place a sleazy kind of feel, but its actually quieter than the Malaysia, less of a 'scene'.

Boston Inn — Soi Si Bamphen, off Soi Ngam Duphli. Singles here are 100B with ceiling fan, 120B for a double. Air-con rooms for 130B single, 150B double. The staff are friendly, rooms are clean. Best value in the Ngam Duphli area.

Banglamphu If you're really on a tight budget, head for Khao San Rd, near the Democracy monument, parallel to Ratchadamnoen Klang Rd — a No. 17 or 56 bus will get you there. Here you will find:

VS Guest House — Two locations, at 136 Tanao Rd (an alley off Khao San Rd) and 1/3 Prachatipotai Rd, near the Thai Hotel. Both 30B per person or double for 60B. Dark and not particularly clean, but adequate.

Bonny Guest House — Khao San Rd, an English sign points the way. 40B per person, several beds per room, fairly clean, friendly proprietors but not much English spoken. The owners plan to add more rooms to the house soon.

Tum (Toom) Guest House — Next door to the Bonny GH and owned by the same family. Also 40B per person, similar arrangement.

New Sri Phranakhorn Hotel — 139 Khao San Rd. 100B per room, single or double, with fan. Chinese-owned, clean.

Nit Jaroen Suke — Next door to New Sri Phranakhorn Hotel on Khao

A Chicken stew vendor, Chieng Mai
B A well-stocked Thai restaurant
C Several varieties of shrimp paste, Chieng Mai

San Rd. A very clean double goes for 100B, with fan and bathroom. Recommended.

Vieng Thai Hotel — 42 Tani Rd, Banglamphu, one street up from Khao San Rd. Over 500B for a double, 370B with student discount. Student Travel Australian has its Bangkok office here.

Chinatown-Hualamphong

Empire Hotel — 572 Yaowarat Rd, near the intersection of Yaowarat and New Rd (Charoen Krung Rd), a short walk from Wat Traimit. Doubles are 120B — a bit noisy but a great location if you like Chinatown. The Empire is a favourite among Thais from the southern region.

Other Chinatown hotels, most without English signs out front, can be found along Yaowarat, Chakraphat, and Ratchawong Rds. The *Burapha*, at the intersection of Chakraphat and Charoen Krung on the edge of Chinatown, is not too bad, rates are about the same as the Empire.

Sri Hualamphong Hotel — 445 Rong Muang Rd. This road is alongside the Hualamphong Railway Station and has several Thai hotels. This is one of the better ones — 80B single, 140 double with fan.

Sahakit Hotel — A few doors down from the Sri Hualamphong towards Rama IV Rd. Rooms from 90B up.

Jeep Sweng — Between the previous two on Rong Muang Rd. Not too clean but adequate, rooms are 70B and up.

No Name Hotel — That is, no name out front, in *any* language. This one's down at the far end of Rong Muang. Pretty basic but 70B for a room.

Watch your pockets/bag around the Hualamphong area, both on the street and on the bus. The cream of the razor artists operates here as the railway passengers make good pickings.

Siam Square Area

Scout Hostel — On Rama I Rd, next to the National Stadium. Dorm beds are 30B per night here.

Star Hotel — 36/1 Soi Kasem San 1, off Rama I Rd. All the way at the end of the *soi*, the Star is a real Thai hotel, with fairly clean, comfortable, air-con rooms with bath for 150-200B for double, depending on the room.

Muangphol Building — On the corner of Soi Kasem San 1 and Rama I Rd. Doubles for 260B. Good value for the discriminating traveller who can afford it — air-con, restaurant downstairs, friendly staff, and good service. Bathrooms have hot water and western-style toilets, both of which function well. Muangphol has the same comfort as, say, the Miami, Viengtai, or Liberty, but is better located and lower priced.

Sukhumwit Area Nothing much can be said for this area — staying here puts you in the newest part of Bangkok and the farthest from the old Bangkok near the river. Buses take longer to get here, and taxis to or from Sukhumwit Rd cost more since it is known as a residential area for *farangs*.

Atlanta — Soi 2 (Soi Phasak) Sukhumwit Rd. Air-con doubles for 180B, rooms with fans for 100B. Not too clean, surly staff.

Miami — Soi 13 Sukhumwit. A favourite among Arab tourists (rivaling the Rajah, Nana and Grace Hotels on Soi 3) who are driving the prices up. A double with fan (only a few available) is 220B, with air-con 300B. Comfortable, clean; includes swimming pool.

Crown — Soi 25 Sukhumwit. Kind of far out of Sukhumwit Rd, but only 174B for a clean, comfortable air-con double — this has a swimming pool too.

EATING IN BANGKOK

There are lots of cheap eating establishments in Banglamphu — most of the noodle shops along Khao San Rd close at night, but around the corner on Ban Tanao Rd are several good places to eat at night.

Across Ratchadamnoen Klang Ave, at the south-east side of the Democracy Monument, is one of Bangkok's best Thai restaurants — the *Sarn Daeng*. Fish is prepared well here, and the restaurant is famous for its *tawt man plaa*, fried fish cakes. Prices are reasonable and I believe there is an English menu available.

Soi Ngam Duphli has several world traveller hangouts, eg the *Lisboa* and *Blue Fox*, both air-con and slightly high-priced since they cater to such western tastes as toast and scrambled eggs. Better are the open-air restaurants on Soi Si Bamphen (near the Boston Inn) which are low to moderate in price, have English menus, and decent food, mostly Thai and Chinese. In this area, the curry shops out on Rama IV are best for cheap nutrition — 7-8B for curry and rice — check the ones near the pedestrian bridge. Also cheap eats can be had across Rama IV in the daily market, look for a cluster of umbrellas.

There is no shortage of cheap places to eat on Rong Muang Rd in Hualamphong, especially if you like north-eastern Thai food — steamed innards and the like.

Excellent foodstalls can be found in the alleys between the Siam Square *sois* — *khao man kai*, or other rice-plates, plus tea, for 7B. The big noodle restaurant on the last *soi*, facing Henri Dunant Rd, called *Co-Co*, is really good for Chinese food. Down the road from Co-Co is a very good Thai restaurant called *Kaeng Thai Rama*. And, of course, the usual assortment of mobile noodle shops abound in the area.

On Sukhumwit try the *Yong Lee Restaurant* at Soi 15, near Asia Books. Excellent Thai and Chinese food and good service at reasonable prices has made Yong Lee a favourite among Thai and *farang* residents alike. There are many restaurants around the major hotels on Sukhumwit with Thai-Chinese-European-American menus, most of average quality and average prices, like the *Number One Restaurant*, good if you're not used to Thai food. Several rather expensive west European restaurants (Swiss, French, German, etc) are also found along tourist Sukhumwit. A few Indian-Pakistani-Middle Eastern restaurants are cropping up on Soi 3 — medium to high prices.

The best Indian restaurant in town, frequented almost exclusively by Indian residents, is the *Royal India* at 392/1 Chakraphat Rd in Pahuraht, the Indian fabric district. It is very crowded at lunchtime, so it might be better to go there after the standard lunch hour or at night. The place has very good *dahl*, curries, Indian breads, *raita* and *lassis*, etc for both vegetarian and non-vegetarian eaters at quite reasonable prices. Definitely a better value than the *Muslim Restaurant* on New Rd, which costs more and has watery curries but has been a traveller's standby. There are at least two more Indian restaurants down alleys off Chakraphat Rd, no names and difficult to find, that are downright cheap. Vegetable *samosas* can be bought in the street in Pahuraht.

On Patphong Rd the *Thai Room*, a Thai-Chinese-Mexican-*Farang* place, is favored by Thai-*farang* couples, Peace Corps volunteers, and off-duty barmaids. Prices are reasonable. If you crave German or Japanese food, there are plenty of places serving these cuisines on and around Patphong Rd. *Bobby's Arms*, an Aussie-Brit pub, has good fish-and-chips.

Out on Silom Rd there are a couple of good restaurants. The medium-priced *Talaad Nam Restaurant* has great Thai food — especially soups and *laap kai* — and is air-conditioned upstairs, open downstairs. The place is nicely decorated in bamboo, with Thai *bongs (ganja* waterpipes), hill-tribe crossbows, etc hanging on the walls. Across the street from the Taalad Nam look for a glassed-in Thai restaurant advertising Singh beer for 28B; inside find two rooms, one air-con, one *au naturel* (sweaty in the hot season) — very good low-priced Thai food with discount beer.

Down Sala Daeng Rd, off Silom, are several different places to eat — noodle shops, street vendors, an ice cream parlour, and the tiny air-con *Irrawaddy Restaurant*, with 'American fried rice' (Thai fried rice with ketchup), 'American breakfasts', but also Thai noodle dishes, and good chicken fried in holy basil.

At the other end of Silom, across from the Narai Hotel is a South Indian (Tamil) temple near which street vendors sell various Indian snacks. Around the corner of Silom on New Rd is the Muslim Restaurant mentioned above. More similar food is available at the *Himali Cha-Cha Restaurant* nearby.

Pratunam, the market district at the intersection of Phetburi and Ratchaprarop, down from the Indra Regent, is a good hunting grounds for Thai food. Check out the big night markets — one a few *sois* up from Phetburi Rd (toward the Indra) on the right side of Ratchaprarop, or another across the street in the alleys behind storefronts on Ratchaprarop. Yet another is located off Phetburi just west of the big intersection on the south side of the road, back behind the storefronts there. These are all great places to eat real Thai food and see 'pure' (non-western) urban Thai culture. The Pratunam markets are open with corrugated tin roofs high above the tables and rustic kitchens, all bathed in flourescent light. The market on the east side of Ratchaprarop is more like a series of connected tents — one specialty there is a tangy fish stomach soup, *kaphaw plaa*. Four people can eat a large meal here, drinking beer or rice whiskey and nibbling away for hours, and only spend around 150-200B, cheaper if it's rice whiskey rather than beer. Night markets in Bangkok, as elsewhere in Thailand, have no menus so you had better have your restaurant Thai in shape before venturing an evening — or better, get a Thai friend to accompany you.

There are several Sala Foremost Ice Cream shops in Bangkok — one at Siam Square, one on Ploenchit Rd, one on Charoen Krung near the Post Office, one on Ratchaprarop Rd in Pratunam, one in Patphong, they're springing up everywhere.

OUTSIDE BANGKOK

Ayuthaya
Most visitors stay at the *U Thong* on U Thong Rd near the boat landing and Chan Kasem Palace. Rooms run from 60B to 120B per night, some are air con. The *Thai Thai*, at 13/1 Naresuan Rd, between Wat Rajburana and the road to Wat Phra Men, has air-con rooms from 80B up. The *Cathay*, near the *U Thong* towards Hua Raw market is 60-80B for a room with a fan.

Best places to eat are the Hua Raw market, on the river near Chan Kasem Palace, and the Chao Phrom market on Chao Phrom Rd east of Wat Rajburana. There are quite a few restaurants on the main road into Ayuthaya, Rojana Rd, and there are two floating restaurants on the Pa Sak River, one on either side of the Pridi Damrong Bridge.

Lopburi
Best visited as a day trip from Ayuthaya. If you must stay for the night try:
Muang Thong — Surasongkhram Rd. 50-100B rooms.
Asia Lopburi — 1/7-8 Surasak Rd. Some rooms air-con, 70-160B.

Nakhorn Pathom
Mitsumphon — Lungphra Rd, near the rail station. 60-100B, some rooms air-con.
Mit Phaisan — Near the west side of Phra Pathom Chedi. Rooms for 60B up with fan.
Sirichai — 37-41 Saiphra Rd, north side of the Chedi. Same rates as the *Mit Phaisan*.
Good eats are available near the railway station.

Kanchanaburi
River Kwai — Down the street (Saengchuto Rd) from the expensive Wang Thong Hotel. Clean and comfortable rooms for 95B with fan.
Si Roong Ruang — 1/2 Tesaban Rd. Doubles with fan 60B up.
Prasobuk Bungalow — Saengchuto Rd. 60-150B.
Luxury — Tambol Ban Neua, north of town, 60-80B.
Muang Thong — Tambol Ban Neua, 80-100B.

Si Racha

If you must spend the night here, there are a couple of cheap but quite adequate hotels on the waterfront near the Si Racha Restaurant; one is built on the piers over the water. Good seafood in this area, too. The TAT runs a hotel in Bangphra, north of Si Racha, with rooms for 80B up.

Koh Si Chang

Try the second floor verandah of Chulalongkorn's abandoned palace or camp on the beach, west and north-west sides of the island.

Pattaya

Cheapest place in town is *Bonanza Lodge* — Soi 15, Pattaya Beach Rd. 60B single, 80B double. Not so clean, noisy, but liveable.

On Soi 13 (next to *Winsand Guest House*) are the *Porn Guest House*, *Super Romantic Guest House*, *Rin GH*, and *Siam GH*, all about 100B for a double.

Pattaya 12 — Soi 12. Very clean and comfortable double rooms with fans on the second floor go for 150B. Air-con rooms are quite a bit more. Best accommodation value in Pattaya.

Most food in Pattaya is expensive, but good Thai food is available in shops along Pattaya's back street (Pattaya No. 2 Rd), away from the beach. Look for cheap rooms for rent back here, too.

Rayong

Rayong O-Thani — 169 Sukhumwit Rd. Rooms for 80B up.
Rayong Hotel — Tha Pradu. Rooms for 60-80B.

Northern Thailand

The first true Thai kingdoms (Sukhothai, Chieng Mai, and Chieng Saen) arose in what is today northern Thailand, hence this region is dotted with great temple ruins. It is also the home of most of the Thai hill tribes whose cultures are dissolving fast in the face of Thai modernization and foreign tourism. The scenic beauty of the North has been fairly well-preserved, though, and Chieng Mai is still probably Thailand's most liveable city.

The northern Thai people in general are known for their relaxed, easy-going manner, which shows up even in their speech — the northern dialect has a slower rhythm to it than Thailand's other three major dialects.

The North also contains the infamous Golden Triangle, the region where Burma, Laos, and Thailand meet, and the source for most of the world's illicit opium. Aside from the air of adventure and mystery surrounding the Golden Triangle, it is simply a beautiful area through which to travel.

CHIENG MAI

710 km north-west of Bangkok. Over 300 temples, almost as many as in Bangkok, fill out Chieng Mai, making it a striking city, visually speaking. Doi Suthep Mount rises 1676 metres above and behind the city, providing a nice setting for this fast-developing city.

Historically, Chieng Mai became the successor to King Mengrai's Chieng Rai kingdom, after he had conquered the post-Dvaravati kingdom of Hari-punchai (modern Lamphun) in 1281. Mengrai, originally a prince of Nan Chao, a Thai kingdom in south-west China, had the city of Chieng Mai ('new city') built from scratch at the foot of Doi Suthep in 1296. Chieng Mai later became a part of the larger Lan Na Thai ('million Thai rice-fields') kingdom, which extended as far south as Kamphaeng Phet and as far north as Luang Prabang in Laos, until captured by the Burmese in 1556. This was the second time the Burmese had control of Chieng Mai province; before Mengrai came along, King Anuruddha of Pagan ruled the area during the 11th century. As a result, Chieng Mai architecture shows a great deal of Burmese influence.

Chieng Mai was recaptured by the Thais under King Taksin in 1775.

Things to See in Chieng Mai

Wat Chieng Man The oldest *wat* in the city, founded by King Mengrai in 1296, features typical northern Thai architecture with massive teak columns inside the *bot*. There is a bas-relief, called Buddha Sila, from Sri Lanka, which is kept locked up here, but which can be seen by request. Also the well-known Crystal Buddha, shuttled back and forth between Siam and Laos like the Emerald Buddha, is kept here.

Wat Phra Singh Begun by King Pa Yo in 1345, the *wiharn* which houses the Phra Singh image was built between 1385 and 1400, and the *bot* was

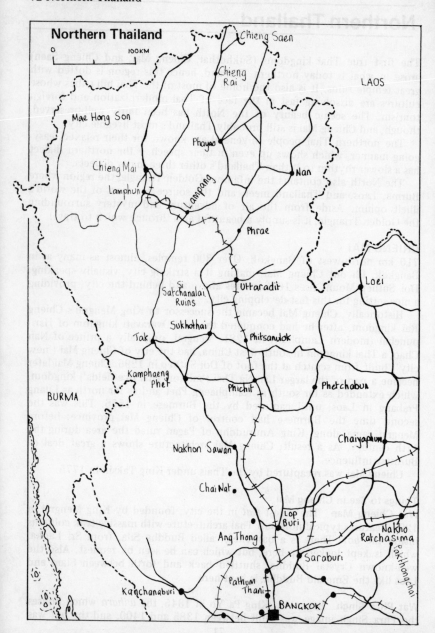

Northern Thailand

0 100KM

Chieng Saen

Chieng Rai

LAOS

Mae Hong Son

Phayao

Nan

Chieng Mai

Lamphun

Lampang

Phrae

Loei

Si
Satchanalai
Ruins

Uttaradit

Sukhothai

Tak

Phitsanulok

Kamphaeng
Phet

Phichit

Phetchabun

BURMA

Chaiyaphum

Nakhon Sawan

Chai Nat

Lop
Buri

Nakho
Ratchasima

Ang Thong

Saraburi

Pak Thongchai

Kanchanaburi

Pathum
Thani

BANGKOK

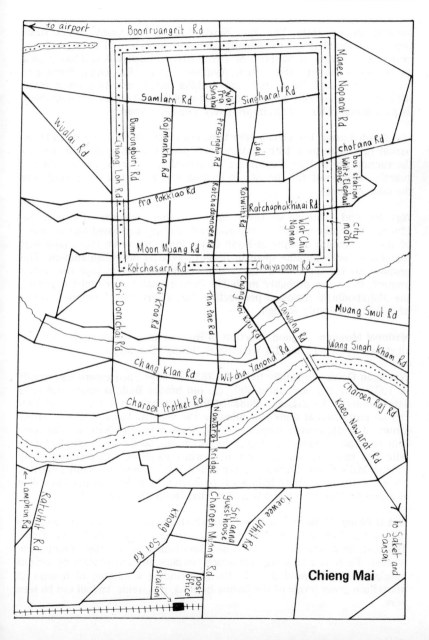

Chieng Mai

finished around 1600. The Phra Singh Buddha supposedly comes from Ceylon, though it is not particularly Sinhalese in style, and since it is identical to two images in Nakhorn Si Thammarat and Bangkok and has quite a travel history behind it (Sukhothai, Ayuthaya, Chieng Rai, Luang Prabang — the usual itinerary for a travelling Buddha image, involving much royal trickery), no one really knows which image is the real one or can document its provenance. This *wat* has impressively well-kept grounds.

Wat Chedi Luang Contains a very large old venerable *chedi*, dated 1441, in partial ruins due to a 16th century earthquake according to some, due to the cannon-fire of King Taksin in 1775 according to others. The *lak muang*, guardian deity-post for the city, is located within the *wat* compound near the main entrance.

Wat Jet Yod Outside of town on the northern highway loop near the Chieng Mai museum. Built in the mid-15th century and based on the design of the Mahabodhi Temple in Bodh Gaya, India, the seven spires represent the seven weeks Buddha spent in Bodh Gaya after his enlightenment. The proportions for the Chieng Mai version are quite different than the Indian original, so it was probably modelled from a small votive tablet depicting the Mahabodhi in distorted perspective. Not a very 'busy' temple in terms of worship, curiously enough.

National Museum A good selection of Buddha images is on display here, in all styles. Open 9-12 and 1-4 Wednesday through Sunday.

Wat Suan Dawk Originally built in 1383, the large open *wiharn* was rebuilt in 1932. The *bot* contains a 500 year old bronze Buddha image and vivid Jataka murals. Amulets and Buddhist literature printed in English and Thai can be purchased at quite low prices in the *wiharn*. There is an interesting group of whitewashed stupas in back, framed by Doi Suthep. The large central stupa contains a Buddha relic which supposedly self-multiplied. One relic was mounted on the back of a white elephant (commemorated by Chieng Mai's White Elephant gate) which was allowed to wander until it 'chose' a site on which to built a *wat* to shelter the relic. It stopped and died at a spot on Doi Suthep and Wat Phra That Doi Suthep was built.

Wat U Mong U Mong is a forest *wat* which has been in use since Mengrai's rule in the 14th century. It is connected to another *wat* in Chaiya, South Thailand, by the influence of Achaan Buddhadasa, a well-known monk and teacher. There is a building here which contains modern artwork by various monks who have resided at U Mong, including a number of *farangs*. A marvellous grisly image of the fasting Buddha, ribs, veins, and all can be seen here.

Chieng Mai Jail Located near the centre of town, off Ratwithi. Come here to see the dozens of *farangs* who have been incarcerated on drug charges. Chieng Mai is notorious for its *samlor* drivers who sell dope and then inform the police on their customers. Fines for even the smallest amounts of *ganja* are very high — 50,000B for a couple of grams is not unusual. Those who cannot afford to buy out of this game go to jail.

Getting Around Chieng Mai
Songthaews go anywhere on their route for 4B. Large city buses are 2B — the TAT office in Chieng Mai has a map with bus routes. *Samlors* should be about 5B for most trips. Far and away the best way to get around Chieng Mai is by bicycle; the city is small enough that all is accessible by bike, including Chieng Mai University, Wat U Mong, Wat Suan Dawk, the National Museum, etc on the outskirts of town. Bikes can be rented for 20-25B per day from several of the guest houses — see Accommodation.

Getting to Chieng Mai
The express train to Chieng Mai from Bangkok leaves Hualamphong station at 6 pm, arriving at 7.30 am the next day. The rapid train leaves daily at 3 pm, arriving 5.20 am. Second class fare is 217B (plus 25B surcharge for the express, 15B for the rapid). Only the Express has sleeping berths available, recommended, 65B for an upper, 95B for a lower. Third class fare, available on the Rapid only, is 104B.

Ordinary buses leave Bangkok's Northern Bus Terminal daily at 5.30 am, 7.25 am, 9.10 am, 10.30 am, 12.30 pm, 1.30 pm, 7.15 pm, 8.45 pm, 9.20 pm, 9.40 pm, and 10 pm. The trip takes eight hours and costs 118B. Air-con 'tour' buses leave from the same terminal at 9.10 am, 10 am, 8.30 pm, 9.10 pm, and 9.30 pm, taking nine hours for a cost of 180B one-way, 320B round trip.

Several private companies in Bangkok run tour buses to Chieng Mai — two are Grand Tour, from Ploenchit Rd, 9 pm, 200B (one-way); and Indra Tour, from the Indra Regent Hotel, 9.30 am and 9 pm, 180B one-way. They all take about nine hours to make the trip.

Buses to Chieng Mai are easy to get out of any of the other northern towns, eg Phitsanuloke, Sukhothai, Lampang, Uttaradit.

Thai Airways flies to Chieng Mai every day at 7.30 am, 8.30 am and 2 pm. On Friday and Sunday there is also a 5.30 pm flight and on every day but Wednesday there is an additional 6.30 pm flight. The flights all take about an hour and the fare is 1100B one-way. There are also flights to Chieng Mai from Chieng Rai, Phitsanuloke, Nan, Phrae, and Mae Hong Son.

OUTSIDE CHIENG MAI
Doi Suthep 16 km north-west of Chieng Mai. Near the summit of Doi Suthep is Wat Phra That Doi Suthep, first established in 1383 under King

Ku Na. A *naga* (dragon-headed serpent) staircase of 300 steps leads to the *wat* at the end of the winding road up the mountain. At the top you can get some fine aerial views of Chieng Mai if the weather is good. Inside the cloister is an intriguing copper-plated *chedi* topped by a five-tier gold umbrella.

Beyond Wat Phra That about five km is *Phu Ping Rajaniwat*, a royal palace, the gardens of which are open on weekends and holidays. The road that passes Phu Ping Rajaniwat splits off to the left, stopping at the peak of Doi Bui. From there a dirt road proceeds for two or three km to a nearby Meo hill tribe village, passable only by motorcycle/jeep or on foot. If you haven't already visited more remote villages, it's worth visiting even though well-toured. Some Meo handiwork can be purchased there and traditional homes and costumes seen. Tall *ganja* plants grow wild in back of the village.

Tribal Research Centre Located on Chieng Mai University campus, five km west of the city. A No. 1 bus goes by the university. The centre features a small hill tribes museum, and literature on hill tribes is available. The staff can help you plan your own hill tribe trip for a lot less cash than tours out of Chieng Mai.

HILL TRIBE TREKS

For years now Chieng Mai has been a centre for treks into the mountainous northern areas inhabited by hill tribes. It used to be pretty exciting to knock about the dirt roads of rural Chieng Rai province, do the boat trip between Fang and Chieng Rai, and hike into the various villages of the Karen, Meo, Akha, and Yao tribes, and the Kuomintang settlements, spending the night in rustic surroundings, perhaps share some opium with the villagers. Only a very few Thais living in Chieng Mai had the travel and linguistic knowledge necessary to lead adventurous foreigners through this area, and booking a trip meant waiting for optimum conditions and number of participants, sometimes quite a while. Alas, the trips began to get increasingly popular in the early 70s and today virtually every hotel and guest house in Chieng Mai books hill tribe tours for countless tour organizations. Soon the word was out that the area north of the Kok River, in the Golden Triangle area, was being 'over-trekked', meaning that various treks were criss-crossing the area in such a fashion that the hill tribe villages were starting to become human zoos. When their only contact with the outside world and with foreigners is through a camera lens and a steady flow of candy and cigarettes, hill tribespeople begin to develop a complex.

So the 'up-to-date' tours moved south of the Kok River, around Chieng Dao and Wieng Papao, where most of them operate today. It's only a matter of time (not much) before this area suffers from the heavy traffic as well. Meanwhile hundreds of foreign travellers continue to take these treks every year, most of them still coming away with a sense of adventure, a few disillusioned. What makes a good trek is, most ·importantly, a good leader-

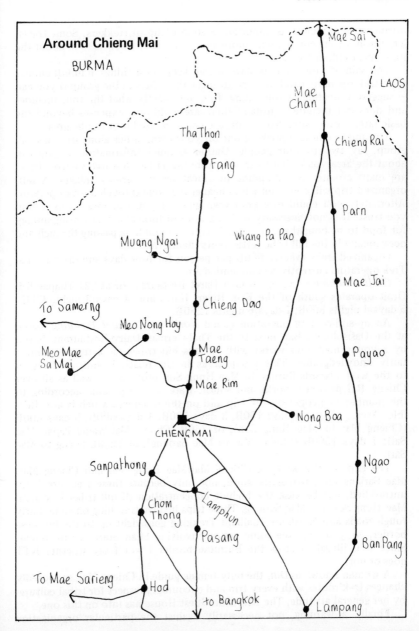

organizer, and, almost as important a good group of trekkers. Some travellers finish a tour complaining more about the other trekkers than about the itinerary, food, or trek leader.

This said, if you want to make a trek keep these things in mind: choose your trek operator carefully, try to meet the others in the group if you can — suggest a meeting or something; find out exactly what the tour includes and does not include — usually there are additional expenses beyond the basic rate. If everything works out, even an organized tour can be great.

You might consider striking out on your own, either alone or in a small group, say two to four people. Gather as much information as you can about the area you'd like to trek in from the Tribal Research Centre. There are maps around that pinpoint the locations of various villages. A self-organized trip will come out a lot cheaper than one through a tour operator. Alternately you could hire your own guide if you can locate one whom you trust. It is not necessary to bring a lot of food along, just bring money for food to be bought in the small Thai towns you'll be passing through and occasionally in the hill tribe settlements themselves.

Organized treks average 600B per person for four days and three nights. Trek operators currently recommended are:

Orbit Trekking — Book through Daret Restaurant or at 221 Thapae Rd. Orbit operates south of the Kok River. Rates are: 4 days/3 nights 600B; 5 days/4 nights 800B; 7 days/6 nights 1250B.

An up-and-coming operation called *Northern Thailand Trekking*, based at the Oasis Jungle Bar, next to the Thai-German Dairy Restaurant, is run by a young man who works with various hill tribes (as a teacher) and is fairly knowledgeable. This group treks in the relatively untoured region to the west towards Burma, in Mae Hong Son province, as well as all over Chieng Rai province, north and south. Rates are negotiable according to the number of people on the trip and on the itinerary, which is also flexible. Average costs: 2 days 400B; 3 days 500B; 4 days 600B; 5 days 800B (Chieng Mai to Mae Hong Son), or 750B (Chieng Mai/Wieng Papao/Mae Sai); 7 days 1500B (Chieng Mai to Mae Sarieng), or 1250B (Fang to Mae Sai).

The trips to the west, eg Chieng Mai/Mae Hong Son and Chieng Mai/Mae Sarieng are particularly good, not only because these areas are fairly untravelled, but because the highest concentration of hill tribes is around Mae Hong Son and Mae Sarieng. These trips involve travelling on some fairly rough roads and Northern Thailand Trekking goes right up to the Burmese border, so you may see some action involving Shan States Army rebels. Since it is illegal to cross the Burmese border I won't say whether NTT does or not.

A woman known as *Din*, the only female guide in Chieng Mai, supposedly changes trek routes with every trip and encourages respect for tribal cultures by her general attitude. The Riverside Guest House has info on this one.

Finally a warning, not necessarily against the particular organization involved, but of possible trends to watch. In April 1981 a group of 10 travellers with *New Wave Treks*, doing a pretty well-worn route, was robbed while hiking between villages by a small band of armed robbers; everything of value was taken, cameras, watches, money, and some clothes, plus there was an attempted rape and a few heads bashed. Some of the persons in the group were thus stranded in northern Thailand until they could get money from home. The bandits were thought to be Karens who hightailed it across the border into Burma with their booty. Authorities in Chieng Mai consider it an isolated incident, but have stepped up hill country patrols.

PHITSANULOKE
389 km from Bangkok. *Wat Phra Si Ratana Mahathat* is the home of the Jinaraj Buddha, one of Thailand's most revered and copied images.

Phitsanuloke is a good starting point for a tour of the north. Check out the markets by the river for bargains on upcountry Thai craft. Besides Wat Mahathat and the markets there is little else to see in Phitsanuloke, but the town has a nice ambience about it.

Getting There
The 6 pm Express to Chieng Mai from Bangkok stops in Phitsanuloke at 12.05 am; the 3 pm Rapid arrives at 8.18 pm. The basic train fare to Phitsanuloke is 122B second class, 60B third.

Ordinary buses leave for Phit from the Northern Bus Terminal in Bangkok at 8.10 am and 9.55 pm, one-way fare is 74B.

Thai Airways flies to Phit daily at 8.30 am, arriving at 9.05 am. The fare is 630B. Phit's airport is a way out of town, but *songthaews* come every 20 minutes or so which will take you all the way to the Nan River for 4B. The big hotels in town also run free buses into town from the airport.

SUKHOTHAI
447 km from Bangkok. Thailand's first capital, flourishing from the mid-13th century to the late 14th century, was Sukhothai. The new town of Sukhothai, however, is undistinguished except for its very good Municipal Market in the centre of town. Old Sukhothai has quite a spread of admirable ruins about 12 km outside of town, making an overnight stay in new Sukhothai worth it. A *tuk-tuk* and driver can be hired for 20-50B an hour (depending on whether you hire them in town or at the old city) and this can save you much time and sore feet in touring the ruins. In addition, guides of varying ages and knowledge hang around hotels and markets in Sukhothai as well as around the ruins. If you have lots of time and stamina you can walk from site to site, though it might take two days to see it all.

It's best to forget seeing the remote ruins of Saphan Hin and others in the hills west of the old city for the time being — even a hired guide will refuse to go there anymore without an armed guard — as there are too many bandits in the hills.

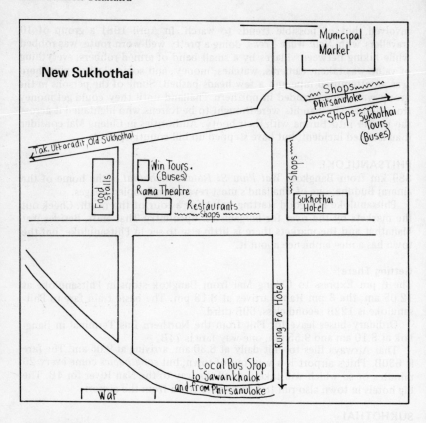

New Sukhothai

Municipal Market

Shops Phitsanuloke

Shops Sukhothai Tours (Buses)

Tak, Uttaradit, Old Sukhothai

Food Stalls

Win Tours. (Buses)

Rama Theatre

Restaurants Shops

Sukhothai Hotel

Rung Fa Hotel

Local Bus Stop to Sawankhalok and from Phitsanuloke

Wat

What to See
Ramkhamhaeng National Museum The museum provides a good starting
point for an exploration of the ruins. Check the well-made miniature model
of the old city and its environs for orientation and relative distances between sites. This will help in planning which sites to visit first and in what
kind of order. A replica of the famous Ramkhamhaeng inscription is kept
here amongst what is a good collection of Sukhothai artifacts. A guide to
the ruins can be purchased here or at the entrance to the ruins of Wat
Mahathat.

A Umbrella painting, Bor Sang near Chieng Mai
B Pattaya Beach

The museum is open 9-12 and 1-4 Wednesday through Sunday. Admission is 2B on weekends, free on weekdays. Certain ruins have 2B admission fees, also.

Wat Mahathat The largest in the city, built in the 13th century, and surrounded by brick walls (206 by 200 metres) and a moat. The spires feature the famous 'lotus-bud' motif of Sukhothai architecture. Some of the original stately Buddha figures still sit among the ruined columns of the old *wiharns*. The *chedis* within the monastery walls number 198 — a lot to explore.

Wat Srisawai Just south of Wat Mahathat stands this 12th-13th century shrine, featuring three corncob-like *prangs* and a picturesque moat. Built by the Khmers as a Hindu temple, originally.

Wat Sra Si Sits on an island west of the Ramkhamhaeng monument. Simple, classic Sukhothai style with one large Buddha, one *chedi*, and the columns of the ruined *wiharn*.

Wat Trapang Thong Next to the museum, this small, still-inhabited *wat* is reached by a footbridge crossing the large lotus-filled pond which surrounds it. This reservoir, the original site of the Loy Krathong festival in Thailand, supplies the Sukhothai community with most of its water.

Wat Phra Pai Luang Outside the city walls to the north and somewhat isolated, this features three Khmer-style *prangs*, like at Srisawai but bigger, dating from the 12th century. This may have been the centre of Sukhothai when it was ruled by the Khmers of Angkor prior to the 13th century.

Wat Si Chum This one is west of the old city and contains the impressive, much-photographed *mondop* with an 11-metre seated Buddha. A passage in the *mondop* wall leads to the top, and Jataka inscriptions line the ceiling of the passage-way — they can only be seen by candle or flashlight.

Wat Chang Lom Off the main highway south of the old city, next to the 'Sukhothai Cultural Centre'. A large *chedi* here is 'supported' by 36 elephants sculpted into its base. There is a good outdoor restaurant between the road and the *wat* which looks expensive but is actually quite reasonable.

Getting There
Sukhothai must be approached from Phitsanuloke. In Phit, take a city bus

A Elephants in the river, on the road to Fang
B Rama I Rd, Bangkok
C Ordination procession, Chainat

(2B) to the *soon*, the 'centre', for buses out of town. If you're coming from the train station or airport you may have to take a minibus to a city bus at the market by the river, then bus to the *soon*. The bus from the *soon* to Sukhothai is 13B, leaves regularly throughout the day, and takes about an hour. A *songthaew* to the old city (*muang kao*) from Sukhothai is 3 or 4B.

Getting out of Sukhothai

Air-con buses to Chieng Mai are run by Win Tours in new Sukhothai and range from 57B to 68B depending on the bus. Sukhothai Tours, out on the main road passing through town, has buses to Chieng Mai for 50B non-air or 70B with air-con. Take the non-air since the air-con doesn't always work on these short-run upcountry tour buses.

Buses to Sawankhaloke and Si Satchanalai leave regularly from the intersection across from the Sukhothai Hotel.

SI SATCHANALAI

The Sukhothai period ruins in Si Satchanalai are pretty much the same as in old Sukhothai — the same basic stylistic range, but some slightly larger sites. Unless you are really a Thai art history buff like me, it would probably be best to choose one of the two cities to explore.

Wat Chedi Jet Thaew Contains seven rows of *chedis*, the largest of which is a copy of one at Wat Mahathat in Sukhothai. There is also an interesting brick and plaster *wiharn* designed to look like a wooden structure (an old Indian technique), with a *prasad* and *chedi* stacked on the roof.

Wat Nang Phya South of Wat Chang Lom. Sinhalese style stupa, built in the 15-16th century.

Wat Chang Lom Same name and style as the one in Sukhothai (elephant-base stupa), but better preserved.

Getting There

The Si Satchanalai ruins are located off the road between new Si Satchanalai and Sawankhaloke. You can either take the Si Satch bus from Sawankhaloke all the way into the new city, and then hire a taxi or minibus back to the ruins, or ask to be let off the bus at the old city (*muang kao*), 12 km short of the new city.

LAMPANG

The site of the city was inhabited as far back as 7th century Dvaravati, and it played an important part in the history of Haripunchai. Many rich Thais have retired here so the *wats* of Lampang are well-endowed. Two typical northern-style temples, Wat Pha Sang and Wat Phra Keo (yes, it once housed the Emerald Buddha, for 32 years, in fact) can be seen on the banks of the

Wang River at the north edge of town.

Wat Lampang Luang, originally constructed during the Haripunchai period but restored in the 16th century, is worth visiting if you can get out to the small town of Koh Kha, about 10 km south-east of Lampang town.

Horse-drawn cabs still ply the streets of Lampang.

Getting There

There is an 8.30 am and 1.30 pm bus to Lampang out of Phitsanuloke's main bus station. From Chieng Mai, your best departure point for Lampang, buses leave out of the 'new' bus station just north of Chang Puak Gate. Fare is 12B.

LAMPHUN

Best seen on a day trip from Chieng Mai, along with Pasang, Lamphun was the centre of the small Haripunchai principality ruled originally by the Mon princess Chama Thevi. Long after Dvaravati, its progenitor, was vanquished by the Khmers, Haripunchai managed to remain independent of both the Khmers and the Chieng Mai Thais.

Wat Phra That Haripunchai is located on the main road into Lamphun from Chieng Mai, on the left. Built in 1157, the *wat* has some interesting post-Dvaravati architecture, a couple of fine Buddha images, and two old *chedis* of the original Haripunchai style.

Another much larger Haripunchai *chedi* can be seen at Wat Chama Thevi (popularly called Wat Kukut), which is said to have been erected in the 9th century — as a Dvaravati monument — but has been restored many times so that it is a mixture of several schools. The stucco standing Buddhas are definitely of the Dvaravati style, but are probably not the original images. Wat Kukut is on the opposite side of town from Wat Haripunchai; walk down the narrow street perpendicular to Chieng Mai-Lamphun Rd (opposite Wat Hari) west, passing over the town moat, passing the district government offices, until you come to Wat Chama Thevi on the left.

Getting There

Buses to Lamphun can be boarded in Chieng Mai on Lamphun Rd near the south side of Nawarat Bridge, and they leave about every 20 minutes throughout the day. The 26-km bus ride, only 5B, proceeds along a beautiful country road, some of it bordered with tall *yang* trees on both sides.

PASANG

A *songthaew* will take you from Lamphun to Pasang (not to be confused with Baw Sang, the 'umbrella village'), a village where cotton-weaving is the cottage industry, for a few baht. The Nantha Khwang shop, one among many that weave and sell their own cotton, is on the right side of the main road going south — recommended for its selection and prices. A well-made cotton shirt of unique Pasang design can be purchased here for 50-60B.

Pasang reputedly has the north's most beautiful women and I must say I can't disagree.

CHIENG RAI

105 km from Chieng Mai. Nothing really to see unless you want to book a hill tribe trek out of Chieng Rai — check with the Chieng Rai Guest House. The town is a bus junction for proceeding on to Mae Chan, Fang, Chieng Saen, and Mae Sai, however.

Getting There

Buses to Chieng Rai can be taken from two places in Chieng Mai — the 'new' bus station, or the bus stop on Lamphun Rd, down a few metres from the Lamphun bus stop near the Nawarat Bridge. Fare varies according to the type of bus but should be about 60B one-way.

Thai Airways has daily flights to Chieng Rai from Chieng Mai International Airport, leaving at 12.30 pm Tuesday, Thursday, and Saturday, 12.55 pm Friday and Sunday, 1.30 pm Monday and Wednesday, for 270B one-way.

MAE HONG SON

368 km, by road, from Chieng Mai. A real crossroad for hill tribes, Burmese immigrants, and the opium trade located in a forested valley. Climb the hill called Doi Kong Mou for a nice view and to see a Burmese-built *wat*. Still peaceful (boring to some) after all these years.

Getting There

The once-daily bus to Mae Hong Son leaves the Chieng Mai Gate on the south side of Chieng Mai at 7 am, and proceeds along a roundabout route which passes through Hot, by Doi Inthanon National Park, and Mae Sarieng along the way, arriving finally in Mae Hong Son about 6 pm. When the government finishes paving the Mae Tang-Pai-Hong Son route the distance by road will only be about 270 km.

Thai Airways makes the trip in 30 minutes for 280B one way, 560B round trip. Flights leave Friday and Sunday at 2.40 pm, Monday and Wednesday at 3.15 pm.

FANG

157 km from Chieng Mai. Fang dates back at least 1000 years as a settlement and trade centre, though the present city was founded by King Mengrai in the 13th century. At least one Yao village and a Karen village can easily be visited from Fang, on your own, and hill tribe treks can also be arranged. A *songthaew* will take you to Tha Ton for 5B where you can get a boat to Chieng Rai down the Kok River; the trip takes at least five hours, leaves around noon, and costs 100B or so, depending on the boat. Accommodation is available at Tha Thon through the Karen Coffee Shop, more inter-

esting than staying in Fang. The proprietor, Phanga, can direct you to other hill tribe settlements in the area.

About 10 km west of Fang at Ban Muang Chom is a system of hot springs, near the Agricultural Station. Just ask for the *baw nam rawn* ('hot water springs'), *baw nam hawn* in northern Thai.

Getting There
Buses to Fang leave from the new bus station north of White Elephant (Chang Puak) Gate. The three-hour trip costs 20B.

MAE SAI
The northernmost town in Thailand, this is a good place to buy Burmese lacquerware, other stuff from Laos and Burma, and to view Akha tribes people. Buses to Mae Sai leave frequently from Chieng Rai for 15B.

CHIENG SAEN
31 km from Chieng Rai. A wonderful little one-street town on the banks of the Maekhong (Mekong) River. The ruins of numerous temples from the Chieng Saen kingdom, stupas, Buddha images, earthen ramparts, and a small museum are there to be admired. The archaeological station behind the museum has a large detailed wall map of Chieng Saen and the surrounding area. Some of the villagers, being Lao immigrants, speak French.

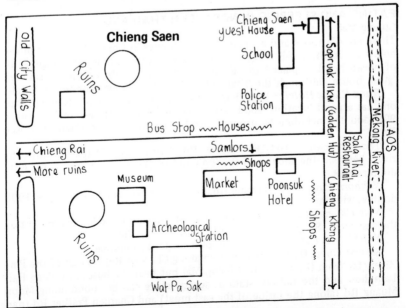

The Laotian side of the mighty Maekhong looks deserted but Lao boats, flying Pathet Lao flags, float by occasionally. Hill tribe crafts can be bought at the Chieng Saen Guest House which is located along the river a few hundred metres up from the police station. About Chieng Saen, Roy Hudson said, 'This is a spot I have a great liking for'.

Farther north 11 km, up the road which runs alongside the river, is Sop Ruak, the official pinnacle of the Golden Triangle, where the borders of Burma, Thailand, and Laos meet, at the junction of the Sop Ruak River and the Maekhong. One bus a day goes to Sop Ruak, in the early morning from the Chieng Saen bus stop, but you can hitch-hike from the front of the Sala Thai Restaurant.

Getting There

The frequent buses from Chieng Rai to Chieng Saen cost 12B and take about 40 minutes.

Returning from Chieng Saen, don't take a Chieng Mai bus (out of Chieng Saen directly) unless you want to travel along the old road, which entails passing through Pham, Payao, Ngao, Lampang, and Lamphun before arriving in Chieng Mai, a nine-hour trip. Bussing first to Chieng Rai (on a Chieng Rai bus, of course) then changing to a Chieng Mai bus which goes along the new road (*sai mai*) makes for a trip of about 4½ hours.

EATING AND SLEEPING IN NORTHERN THAILAND
Chieng Mai

There are 45 hotels and at least 15 guest houses in Chieng Mai. Most of the hotels are in the 300B range — and the guest houses in the 50B range. A lot of cheap hotels replaced the English word 'hotel' with the new flashword 'guest house', although the Thai still reads 'hotel!' Some economical hotels:

Rung Ruang Hotel — 398 Thapae Rd, near the east side of the moat. This one has a good location, good service, clean rooms with fan for 70B single, 90B double, including bathroom. Also has an entrance on Chang Moi Kao Rd.

Thai Charoen — 164-166 Thapae Rd. Farther out Thapae towards the river, between the moat and the TAT office. Singles with fan go for 60B, doubles 80B.

Nakhorn Ping — 43 Taiwang Rd, near the Prince Hotel. 80B single, 100B double, with fan.

New Chieng Mai — 22 Chaiyaphum Rd. Nice hotel, well located right on the east moat. Single with fan, 116B, doubles, 140-200B.

YMCA — 2/4 Mengrai-Rasni Rd. 80B single, 120 double.

Several Guest Houses are clustered along Charoen Raj Rd east of the Ping River, far from the centre of Chieng Mai but near the buses to Chieng Rai/Lamphun and the railway station; several more can be found along Moon Muang Rd (along the inside of the east moat) and Charoen Prathet Rd (parallel to Charoen Raj, but west of the Ping River). All of the guest houses listed below I've checked out and found to be adequate:

Je T'aime Guest House — 247 Charoen Raj Rd. 16 rooms; 50B single, 60B double.

Manit Guest House — 84 Charoen Raj Rd. 9 rooms; 30B single, 60B double.

Mee Guest House — 193 Charoen Raj Rd. 12 rooms; 25B single, 40B double.

Aussie Guest House — 4 Charoen Prathet Rd. 4 rooms; 30B single, 40B double.

Chieng Mai Guest House — 91 Charoen Prathet Rd. The original — 18 rooms; 70-140B per room. A favourite among old Thai hands.

Chumpol Guest House — 89 Charoen Prathet Rd. 21 rooms; 50B single. 80B double.

PK Guest House (Puang Keo Guest House) — Moon Muang Rd near Montri Hotel. 16 rooms; 30B single, 50B double.

Thai-German Guest House — 33 Moon Muang Rd. 9 rooms, 40B single, 60B double.

Orchid Guest House — 22 Moon Muang Rd. 11 rooms; 30B single, 40B double.

Pata Guest House — Soi 6 Moon Muang Rd. Nice place, 8 rooms; 30B single, 50B double.

Saitum Guest House — Moon Muang Rd, behind the Thai-German Dairy Restaurant. 10-11 (?) rooms; 40B single, 50B double.

Chang Moi Guest House — 29 Chang Moi Kao Rd (behind the Chieng Mai Hotel). Good value, beautiful house with garden, clean and comfortable, 5 rooms; 50B single, 60B double.

Sri Lanna Guest House — 55 Taewee Uthit Rd, off Charoen Muang Rd, between river and railway station. 40B single, 70B double.

Chieng Mai Youth Hostel — 302 Manee Noparat Rd, along the north moat. 30B dorm/40B single/60B double.

Eating in Chieng Mai

Daret Restaurant, Thai-German Dairy Restaurant, and *Ban Klai Steak House* are where all the world travellers hang out to eat western food and drink fruit smoothies, though the *Daret* cooks up some pretty fair Thai dishes as well. These restaurants are beside the inside of the east moat. Two good Thai restaurants are just across the moat, the big open-air *Aroon Rai*, specializing in northern Thai dishes, and the smaller but better *Thanarm Restaurant*, between the New Chieng Mai Hotel and Thapae Gate. There is a cheap Chinese restaurant on Chang Moi Rd near the intersection of Chang Moi and Chaiyaphum. *Pat's* is no longer in business, for you old-timers.

The night market on Chaiyaphum Rd, north of the intersection with Chang Moi, has very good food of all kinds at very reasonable prices.

Several open-air restaurants serving north-eastern food (*kai yang, som-*

tam, etc) are clustered around the inside north-eastern corner (a coincidence?) of the city moat, including one place that sells large bottles of Singh beer with meals for 27B each, possibly the cheapest anywhere in Thailand.

Just west of town, on the road to Wat Suan Dawk, Wat U Mong, and Chieng Mai University, is the *Vegetarian Restaurant (raan ahaan mangsawirat)*, which has excellent vegetarian Thai food, using lots of bean curd, mushrooms, and coconut milk, at very low prices — all dishes are 5B each, drinks and desserts 3B each. The *kluay buat chee*, bananas in sweet coconut milk, is particularly tasty.

Phitsanuloke
Near the railway station on Phyalithai Rd (off ChaoPhya Rd where the flashy Amarin Nakhorn Hotel is located), are two economical hotels, the *Hor Fah* and the *Unhachak*. Both have rooms for 70B up. Close by are several cheap restaurants and the market by the Nan River has good food, too, particularly in the early mornings.

Sukhothai
Sukhothai Hotel — 15/5 Singhawat Rd. Around the corner from the town centre, near incoming buses and buses to Sawankhalok. The sign out front has the hotel name in English as well as Thai and Chinese. Nice people in charge. Fairly clean doubles go for 60 to 70B.

Rung Fa — 8 Singhawat Rd. Difficult to find, near the Yom River. Same prices and quality as the Sukhothai.

Sawastipong — 56/2 Singhawat. Other side of town centre, near the municipal market. Grubby rooms for 50B up.

The night market across from Win Tour and the municipal market near town centre both have plenty of places to eat. The restaurant attached to the Sukhothai Hotel is pretty good. There are a couple of restaurants on the road between the Sukhothai Hotel and Win Tour, near the Rama cinema.

Chieng Rai
Chieng Rai Guest House — 717/2 Srikerd Rd, near the main bus station. Doubles from 30B up.

Rama Hotel — 331/4 Traimit Rd. In the centre of town, a couple of blocks from the clock tower, next to Wat Moon Muang, the Rama has clean rooms from 80B up. Restaurants, night clubs, theatres, are located nearby.

Chieng Rai Hotel — Suksathit Rd near the clock tower and district government buildings. Similar to the Rama in rates and quality.

Sukniran — 424/1 Bunpakarn Rd. Between the clock tower and Wat Ming Muang, around the corner from the Chieng Rai Hotel. Air-con rooms from 90B.

There are plenty of restaurants in Chieng Rai, especially along Trairat Rd.

Mae Hong Son

Hotels in Mae Hong Son are all located along its two perpendicular main streets, Singhanat (running east-west) and Khunrun Prapat Rd (north-south). The *Sa-nguan Sin*, 35 Singhanat Rd, is good and has rooms from 60B.

The *Suk Somchai*, on the same road, is more expensive, but has air-con rooms. The *Mitniyom*, on Khunrun Prapat towards Doi Kong Mou, has similar rates and accommodation.

Fang

Best hotel in town is the *Fang Hotel*, with rooms from 50B, if you must stay in Fang. Cheaper rooms can be had at the *Si Sukit*. Nearby Tha Torn, where the boat to Chieng Rai originates, has accommodation at the *Karen Coffee Shop*.

Chieng Saen-Sop Ruak

A choice of three places to stay await the visitor who makes it this far. In Sop Ruak, 11 km north of Chieng Saen along the Maekhong, is the isolated *Golden Hut*, your typical tropical bungalow. If you aren't able to get to Sop Ruak, there is the *Chieng Saen Guest House* in Chieng Saen, on the road to Sop Ruak. Chieng Saen Guest House and the Golden Hut are run by the same family, both cost only 20B per person, single or double, per night. Both sell Burmese and Laotian handicrafts. If these two are full, a good possibility, the only other choice is the *Poonsuk Hotel*, a bright blue ramshackle building (no English sign) near the end of Chieng Saen's main street, towards the river. A double is 50B and mosquito nets are provided. Hill tribes passing through Chieng Saen stay at this hotel, as well as Laotian refugees, so staying here can be an interesting experience.

North-East Thailand

In many ways the north-eastern region of Thailand is the kingdom's 'heartland'. The older Thai customs remain more intact here than elsewhere in the country; partly as a function of the general non-development of the area, the north-east has hosted less tourism. Sites of historical and archaeological significance abound in the north-east, several of which have been restored or excavated recently, so that visitors are finally beginning to 'discover' north-eastern travel. The pace here is slower, the people friendlier, and inflation less effective in the provinces known collectively as *Isaan*, than in Thailand's other major regions.

The term *Isaan* is also used to classify the local people (*khon isaan*) and the local food (*ahaan isaan*), and comes from the Sanskrit name for the Mon-Khmer kingdom Isana, which flourished in the area of (what is now) north-eastern Thailand and pre-Angkor Cambodia. A mixture of Lao and Khmer influence is a mark of Isaan culture and language. The Khmers have left behind several Angkor Wat-like monuments near Surin, Khorat, Buriram and other north-eastern towns, and near the Maekhong River/Lao border in the town of That Phanom is the famous Lao-style temple Wat That Phanom. Many of the people living in this area speak Lao or a Thai dialect which is very close to Lao. Isaan food is famous for its pungency and choice of ingredients. Well-known dishes include *kai yang*, roast spiced chicken, and *som tam*, a spicy salad made with grated unripe papaya, lime juice, garlic, fish sauce, and fresh red pepper. North-easterners eat glutinous rice with their meals, rolling the almost translucent grains into balls with the hands.

The music of the north-east is also highly distinctive in its folk tradition, using instruments like the *khaen*, a reed instrument with two long rows of bamboo pipes strung together, the *pong lang*, a xylophone-like instrument made of short wooden logs, and the *pin*, a small three-stringed lute of sorts played with a large plectrum. The most popular song forms are of the *luk tung* ('children of the fields') type, a very rhythmic style in comparison to the classical music of central Thailand.

The best silk in Thailand is said to come from the north-east, around Khorat (Nakhorn Ratchasima) and Roi Et. A visit to north-eastern silk-weaving towns can produce bargains as well as an education in Thai weaving techniques for those interested.

For real antiquity, Udorn province offers prehistoric cave drawings, at Ban Phu, north of Udorn Thani, and the recently discovered ancient ceramic and bronze culture at Ban Chieng to the east. This latter site, excavated by the late Chester Gorman and his team of University of Pennyvania anthropologists, may prove to be the remains of the world's oldest agricultural society and bronze metallurgy, predating developments in the Tigris-Euphrates valley and in China by centuries.

Main transportation lines (train and bus) in the north-east are along the routes between Bangkok and Nong Khai, and between Bangkok and Ubon

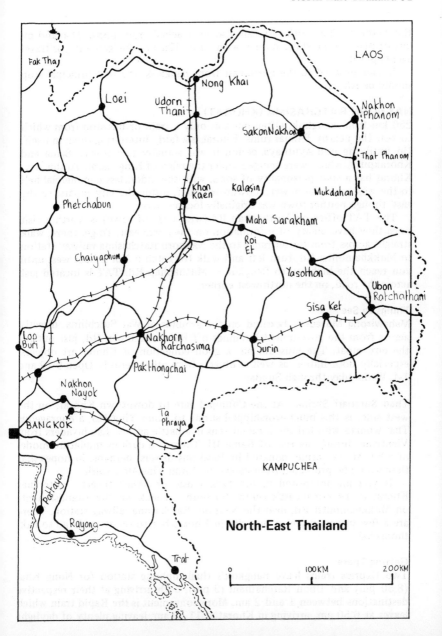

North-East Thailand

Ratchathani. The north-east can also be reached from north Thailand by bus or plane from Phitsanuloke, with Khon Kaen as the 'gateway', as travel agents put it.

If you proceed to the north-east from Bangkok, the first principal stop should be Khorat.

NAKHORN RATCHASIMA (KHORAT)

250 km from Bangkok. Often cited as only a train or bus stop from which to visit the nearby Phimai ruins, Khorat is a fairly interesting town in itself. Up until the mid-Ayuthaya period it was actually two towns, Sema and Khorakpura, which were merged under the reign of King Narai. To this day, Khorat has a split personality of sorts, with the older, less commercial half to the west, and the newer, 'downtown' half, inside the city moats, to the east, though neither town was originally located here.

The TAT office on Mitthaphap Rd (west edge of town) is worth a visit since they have plenty of information on the north-east. To get there, walk straight across from the entrance to the Nakhorn Ratchasima railway station to Mukkhamontri Rd, turn left and walk (or catch a No. 2 bus) west until you reach the highway to Bangkok — Mitthaphap Rd. TAT is located just across the road, on the north-west corner.

Things to See

Mahawirong Museum Located on the grounds of Wat Sutchinda, directly across from the government buildings off Ratchadamnoen Rd, just outside the city moat. The museum has a good collection of Khmer art objects, especially door lintels, as well as objects from other periods. Open 9-12 and 1-4, Wednesday through Sunday.

Thao Suranari Shrine At the Chumpol gate to downtown Khorat, on the west side, is this much-worshipped shrine to Khun Ying Mo, a courageous Thai woman who led the local citizens in a battle against Lao invaders from Vientiane during the rule of Rama III. There is a curious miniature model of a bus at the shrine, donated by local bus drivers, perhaps, in hopes that they would be protected from danger by Khun Ying Mo's spirit.

If you are interested in *luk tung* music or *likhee* theatre, note that Khorat is the north-east's centre for both — check out the establishments on Mukkhamontri Rd, near the Nakhorn Ratchasima railway station. There are a few places to see or buy silk in Khorat but to see it made go to Pakthongchai.

Getting There

Two Express trains leave Bangkok's Hualamphong station for Nong Khai (8.30 pm) and Ubon Ratchathani (9 pm), both arriving at their respective destinations between 1 and 2 am. More convenient is the Rapid train which leaves at 6.50 am, arriving in Khorat at 11.49 am, leaving plenty of daylight

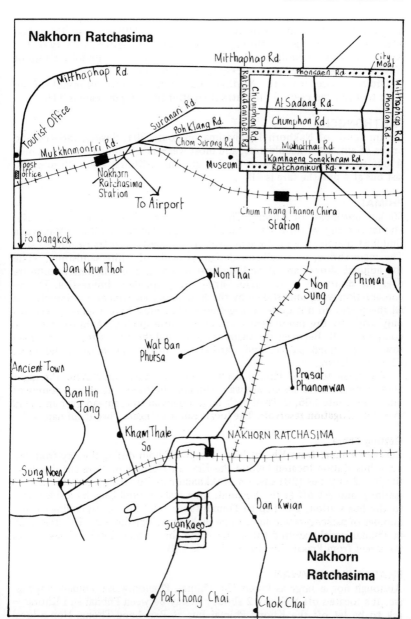

Nakhorn Ratchasima

Mitthaphap Rd.

Mitthaphap Rd.

Phonsaen Rd.

City Moat

At Sadang Rd.

Chumphon Rd.

Mahatthai Rd.

Kamhaeng Songkhram Rd.

Ratchanikun Rd.

Mitthaphap Rd.

Phonlan Rd.

Ratchadamnoen Rd.

Chumphon Rd.

Tourist Office

Suranari Rd.

Poh Klang Rd.

Chom Surang Rd.

Mukkhamontri Rd.

post office

Nakhorn Ratchasima Station

To Airport

Museum

Chum Thang Thanon Chira Station

To Bangkok

Dan Khun Thot

Non Thai

Non Sung

Phimai

Wat Ban Phutsa

Ancient Town

Prasat Phanomwan

Ban Hin Tang

Kham Thale So

NAKHORN RATCHASIMA

Sung Noen

Dan Kwian

Suan Kaeo

Around Nakhorn Ratchasima

Pak Thong Chai

Chok Chai

in which to explore the town. Second class fare is 89B one-way, third class 44B. The train trip passes through some great north-eastern scenery on the Khorat plateau, including a view of the enormous white Buddha figure of Wat Theppitak situated on a thickly forested hillside.

Ordinary buses leave the Northern Bus Terminal every 20 minutes from 5 am to 4 pm and every 30 minutes thereafter to 9.30 pm. Fare is 41B.

PAKTHONGCHAI

28 km south of Nakhorn Ratchasima on route 304. Several varieties and prices of silk are available here, and most weavers sell directly to the public. A bus to Pakthongchai leaves the bus station in Khorat every 30 minutes, last bus at 4 pm; the fare is 6B.

PHIMAI

60 km north-east of Khorat. The 12th century Khmer shrine called Hin Phimai is really worth a visit. Built by King Jayavarman VII as a Mahayana Buddhist temple, the monument projects a majesty that transcends its size. The main shrine, of cruciform design, is made of white sandstone, while the adjunct shrines are of pink sandstone and laterite. The lintel sculpture over the doorways to the main shrine are particularly impressive. The re-construction work undertaken by the Fine Arts Department is complete and all the pieces do not quite fit together as they must have originally, yet this only adds to the monument's somewhat eerie quality. Admission to the complex is 2B. Between the main entrance and the main street of the small town is a ruined palace, and, farther on, an open-air museum featuring Khmer sculpture.

The small town of Phimai itself is nothing much but staying the night here seems rather pleasant anyway. Outside the town entrance, a couple of km down route 206, is Thailand's largest banyan tree, spread over an island in a state irrigation reservoir. The locals call it *sai ngam*, 'beautiful banyan'.

Getting There

Buses to Phimai from Khorat leave every half hour during the day from the main bus station located behind the Erawan Hospital on Suranari Rd. Take the No. 2 city bus (2B) east on Mukkhamontri Rd (right from the railway station), and get off at the hospital; then walk around back by a side street to the bus station. The trip to Phimai takes 1-1½ hours, depending on the number of passengers that have to be picked up along the way. The 'terminal' in Phimai is right around the corner from the Phimai Hotel and just down the street from Prasat Hin Phimai. Fare is 12B.

PRASAT PHANOMWAN

Although not as large as Prasat Hin Phimai, Phanomwan is equally impress-ive. It's located off highway 2 about halfway between Phimai and Khorat — ask to be let off the Khorat-Phimai bus at Ban Long Thong. Hop a local *songthaew*, hitch-hike, or walk the six km through Ban Long Thong and Ban Makha, both knife-making villages, to get to Prasat Phanomwan. Though basically unrestored, Phanomwan is an in-worship temple with resident monks.

UDORN THANI
561 km from Bangkok. Udorn is one of three north-eastern cities (including Ubon and Khorat) that boomed virtually overnight when an American military base was established in each during the US-Vietnam war. Except for nearby Ban Chieng, Udorn has nothing much to offer unless you've spent a long time already in the north-east and seek 'western' amenities like air-conditioned coffee houses, flashy ice cream and massage parlours (no, not together), or *farang* food.

The digs at Ban Chieng village, about 50 km to the east, are interesting to see, and a full-fledged exhibit is currently being developed there. The local villagers occasionally attempt to hawk Ban Chieng artifacts, real and faked — neither type will be allowed out of the country.

There are also some infrequently visited caves with prehistoric wall paintings located in Ban Phue district, 35 km north-west of Udorn.

Getting There
The Express train for Nong Khai leaves Bangkok at 8 pm each day, arriving in Udorn at 7.01 am. The second class fare is 169B, third class 81B. A sleeping berth, recommended for this long trip, is available only in second class for the usual charge, 65B for an upper berth, 95B for a lower. Nice trip.

Buses leave Bangkok's Northern Terminal daily at 8.59 am, 9.29 am, 9.59 am, 11.05 am, 11.10 am, 12.35 pm, 2.50 pm, 4.25 pm, 5.20 pm, 6.10 pm, 7 pm, 7.40 pm, 9.42 pm, 10.30 pm, and 11.10 pm. Fare for the 11-12 hour trip is only 83B.

Thai Airways flies to Udorn on Tuesdays, Thursdays, Fridays, and Sundays from Don Muang at 9 am, arriving Udorn at 10.50 am; there is also a Monday flight leaving at 12.50 pm, arriving in Udorn at 1.35 pm. One-way fare is 750B if you take the Tuesday, Thursday, Friday or Sunday flight, on an Avro 748, and 870B Mondays, when a Boeing 737-200 makes the trip.

From Khorat, buses leave the main bus station for Udorn every half hour during the day, arriving 3½ hours later for a cost of 35B.

To Ban Chieng Take a *samlor* or *songthaew* from Udorn to the *talaat isaan* ('north-eastern market'), off the eastbound highway to Sakhon Nakhorn, for about 5B. From the market hop a *songthaew* bound for Ban Chieng and settle back for the 1-1½ hour trip; fare on this leg is 10B.

KHON KAEN
450 km from Bangkok. A stopping-off place between Khorat and Udorn,

Khon Kaen is about a 2½-hour bus trip from either point. It is also the gateway to the north-east if you are coming from Phitsanuloke in northern Thailand by bus or plane. Khon Kaen, a medium-sized town, boasts a university and a very good provincial branch of the National Museum. The latter features some Dvaravati objects, *sema* stones from Kalasin, and bronze/ceramic artifacts from Ban Chieng. On the banks of Khon Kaen's large (in the rainy season) lake is a venerable north-eastern style *wat*, with elongated spires on the *prasad*, typical for this area.

Khon Kaen is also well-known as the principal place where 'Thai sticks' are assembled. That portion of the product that does not leave town for bigger markets is reputed to be the very best available, in other words, the locals keep the best for themselves — old Thai hands call it 'Khon Kaen Crippler'.

Getting There

The Phitsanuloke-Khon Kaen road runs through spectacular scenery, including a couple of National Parks. Check at the main bus station in Phit for departures and fares, which vary according to type of bus and routing.

Thai Airways flies the Phit-Khon Kaen route on Monday, Wednesday, and Saturday, leaving Phit at 10.50 am, arriving in Khon Kaen at 12.05 pm. The flight going the opposite direction, Khon Kaen to Phit, departs on the same days at 8.45 am, arriving in Phit at 10 am. One-way fare in either direction is 470B.

Buses leave Khorat for Khon Kaen at 5.30 am, 6 am, and 6.30 am, arriving 2½ hours later for 24B. A deisel railcar train leaves Khorat daily at 2.45 pm for a 6.04 arrival in Khon Kaen. Third class fare for the 186 km trip is 35B, twice that for second class.

The Nong Khai Express train, leaving Bangkok at 9 pm, arrives in Khon Kaen at 5.17 am. The Rapid leaves at 6.10 am and arrives at 2.36 pm. The basic fare for either is 138B second class, 67B third. Only the Express has sleepers.

A direct Thai Airways flight departs Bangkok Mondays, Wednesdays, and Saturdays at 7.15 am, landing in Khon Kaen at 8.25 am; one-way fare is 610B.

NONG KHAI

624 km from Bangkok; 55 km from Udorn. Nong Khai is where Route 2, the Friendship Highway, ends, right at the Maekhong River. Across the river is Laos, and Nong Khai is the only point open along the Thai-Lao border

A	A Inland sea at Songkhla
B	B Cotton weaving at Koh Yaw, Songkhla

when the border is open between infrequent skirmishes. Check with the Lao embassy in Bangkok for the possibility of getting a visa for a visit to Vientiane, 20 km north-west of Nong Khai. The Immigration office in Nong Khai itself may be helpful, too. You can take a ferry across to Tha Deua in Laos if your visit is approved, and then catch a taxi to Vientiane.

Getting There

Trains for Nong Khai leave Udorn at 4.50 am, 7.06 am, 4.36 pm, and 8.12 pm, arriving at Nong Khai at 5.40 am, 7.55 am, 5.25 pm, and 9.05 pm. Third class fare is 10.50B.

The Nong Khai Express from Bangkok leaves Hualamphong at 9 pm, arriving in Nong Khai at 7.55 am. There is also a Rapid train which departs at 6.10 am, pulling up in Nong Khai at 5.25 pm. The basic fare is 184B second class, 88B third class one-way; round-trip is 331B second, 158B third. Sleepers are available on the Express.

The long bus trip to Nong Khai from Bangkok costs 91B and buses leave at 4.15 am, 5.15 am, 6.09 am, 6.49 am, 7.19 am, 7.59 am, 8.29 am, and 7.40 pm, 8.10 pm, and 8.54 pm. Buses from Khorat leave at 2 pm, 2.40 pm, 3.20 pm, 4 pm, 4.40 pm, 5.20 pm, 6 pm, and 7 pm; the trip takes four hours and costs 41B.

LOEI

557 km from Bangkok. For outdoors-people there is 1500-metre Phu Kradung mountain about 50 km south-east of Loei city, in Loei province. The mountain, with its large plateau at the top, is a national park with government owned cabins and mapped trails. The main trail scaling Phu Kradung is five km long — porters can be arranged to carry your gear to the top. The climate in Loei province is generally cooler than the rest of Thailand, especially at the top of Phu Kradung.

Getting There

Buses from Bangkok's Northern Bus Terminal leave at 4.32 am, 5.32 am, 7.27 am, 2.03 pm, and 9.30 pm. Fare is 83B. From Udorn buses to Loei leave regularly throughout the day for 25B. From Phitsanuloke you can get a bus to Loei for 65-80B, depending on the bus.

THAT PHANOM

A village lying between Nakhorn Phanom to the north and Mukhadan to the south, That Phanom is famous for its highly revered Lao-style temple, *Wat*

A
B

A Beach on Koh Samui
B Bridge over the River Kwai

That Phanom, similar in form to Wat That Luang in Vientiane. This is a very remote part of the north-east, on the Maekhong, recommended for the adventurous.

Getting There

Buses from Bangkok leave the Northern Bus Terminal for the 729 km trip at 5.45 am, 7.39 am, 8.19 am, 9.26 pm, 10.10 pm and 10.35 pm; fare is 107B. That Phanom can also be approached by bus from Udorn or Ubon Ratchathani.

UBON (UBOL) RATCHATHANI

575 km from Bangkok. One of the bigger cities in the north-east, thanks to the former US military presence there. There is a monastery at nearby Warin Chamrap, called Wat Ba Pong, which has a large contingent of foreign monks studying with Achaan Cha, a well-known Thai monk.

Getting There

The Ubon Ratchathani Express leaves daily from Bangkok's Hualamphong station at 8.30 pm, arriving in Ubon at 6.35 am. There are also two Rapid trains daily at 6.50 am and 6.50 pm, which arrive at 5.25 pm and 5.10 am. Second class fare is 171B, third is 82B.

Buses for Ubon leave the Northern Bus Terminal in Bangkok fifteen times a day between 4.30 am and 11.20 pm. Fare is 100B.

YASOTHORN

This one is difficult to get to, but if you happen to be in the area (say, in Ubon) in the month of May, it might be worth a two-hour bus trip (from Ubon) to catch the annual rocket festival 8-10 May. The rocket festival, prevalent throughout the north-east as a rain/fertility rite, is celebrated most fervently in Yasothorn where it involves a fantastic fireworks display. The name of the town, which has the largest Muslim population in the north-east, comes from the Sanskrit *Yasodhara* for 'preserver or maintainer of glory', the name of one of Krishna's sons by Rukmini in the Mahabharata.

A bus to Yasothorn from Ubon should be in the 25B-30B range.

SURIN

452 km from Bangkok. A forgettable town except during the 'Elephant-Round-up' in late November each year. At that time a carnival atmosphere reigns with elephants providing the entertainment. If ever you wanted to see a lot of elephants in one place (there are more elephants now in Thailand than in India), this is your chance.

Getting There

Surin buses leave daily from Bangkok's Northern Bus Terminal at 6.30 am, 8.30 am, 10.40 am, 1.09 pm, 9.35 pm, and 10.15 pm for 68B. During 'round-up' time there are also many special air-con buses to Surin from major hotels and tour companies.

The best way of all to get to Surin is on the Ubon Ratchathani Express, which leaves Bangkok at 8.30 pm, arriving in Surin at 4.14 am, or the 6.50 am Rapid train, which arrives at 2.48 pm. The basic fare for either train is 63B for third class and 130B for second class. Book your seats at least two weeks in advance during November.

EATING & SLEEPING IN NORTH-EAST THAILAND
Khorat (Nakhorn Ratchasima)
Visit the TAT office in Khorat — they not only give you a map and complete list of hotels, but names of night clubs, restaurants, theatres and 'Turkish baths'. Recommended hotels:

Fah Sang — 68-70 Mukkhamontri Rd, not far from the railroad station. Clean rooms, friendly staff. Singles 75B, doubles 150B. *Poh Thong* — 167-8 Poh Klang Rd. Rooms for 50-80B. Noisy but liveable, near Ratchadamnoen Rd. *Siri Hotel* — 167-8 Poh Klang Rd. A couple of blocks west of the Poh Thong Hotel and city moats. Good location, quiet, friendly. Rooms for 60B up.

Damrongrak — 1674/1 Chumphon Rd, inside the city moats. 70B single, 100B double. *Thai Pokaphan* — 104-6 Atsadang Rd, inside the city moats, across the street from the expensive Khorat Hotel, CP Turkish Bath, near Charoen Rath Theatre, post office. Same rates as the Damrongrak. *Cathay* — 3692/5-6 Ratchadamnoen Rd. Cheap (60-80B) but a bit out of the way. *Khorat Hotel* — Atsadang Rd. 100-150B single, 200B double.

Khorat has many excellent Thai and Chinese restaurants, especially along the western gates to downtown Khorat, near the Thao Surinari Shrine. The curry shops across from the railway station are also very good, and cheap. The best pineapple curry I've eaten in Thailand I found in one of these latter stalls.

Phimai
Only one hotel in town, right around the corner from the bus terminal — *Phimai Hotel.* A very clean and comfortable room is 50B without bath, 80B with. The restaurant next door is very good.

Udorn Thani/Ban Chieng
There are as yet no hotels in Ban Chieng, you must stay in Udorn. Recommended are: *King Hotel* — 57 Pho Sri Rd. 60-110B, some air-con rooms, some with fan. *Thailand* — 4/5 Surakorn Rd, near bus station. Clean rooms, 50-100B. *Victory* — 60 Pho Sri Rd. 50-90B. *Suphanit* — 12/14 Surakorn Rd, near bus station, Thailand Hotel. 45-60B.

There are plenty of places to eat in Udorn, including some with 'western' food. Several restaurants specialize in *ahaan isaan* here.

Khon Kaen

Roma Hotel — 50/2 Klang Muang Rd. 80-150B, all air-con rooms. Good bargain. *Sawatdi* — 177-9 Na Muang Rd. 60-140B. *Khon Kaen Bungalow* — Sri Chan Rd. 60-120B, air-con. *Ban Phai* — 396 Chan Prasit Rd. 40-120B.

Nong Khai

Phong Wichit — Bantherngchit Rd. 50-70B. *Sooksan Motel* — 1164 Prachak Rd. 50-100B, some air-con rooms.

Loei

Thai Udom — 41 Charoen Rath Rd. 60-120B. *King's Hotel* — 11/9 Chumsai Rd. Best deal in town, 70-180B.

Nakhorn Phanom

This is the nearest place to stay for a visit to That Phanom. *Chakawan* — 676/204 Apibarn Bancha Rd. 70B per room. *Lucky* — next door to Chakawan. 70B per room. *Charoensuk* — 692/45 Bamrung Muang Rd. 60B per room. *Nakhorn Phanom Hotel* — 528/39 Apibarn Bancha Rd. 120-200B, all air-con rooms.

Ubon Ratchathani

Ratchathani — 929 Khuan Thani Rd. Rooms from 100-180B, air-con. *Krung Thong* — 24 Sri Narong Rd. Similar rates and accommodation to Ratchathani. *Ubon Siklom* — 22/2 Ubonsak Rd. 60-70B per room. *Ubon Pattana* — 333 Khuan Thani Rd. 70-120B. *Bordin* — 14 Phalochai Rd. 100-180B. *Tokyo* — 178 Upharat Rd. 100-180B. *Siam* — 94 Phalochai Rd. 100-180B; some rooms a little cheaper. *New Nakhorn Luang* — 66-70 Yutthaphan Rd. 60-90B.

Yasothorn

Udomporn — 169 Uthairamrit Rd. 50-80B. *Surawit* — 128/1 Changsanit Rd. 50-120B, air-con. *Yothnakhorn* — 169 Uthairamrit Rd. 70-150B, air-con.

Surin

Hotel rates may increase during the elephant round-up and hotels may fill up. *Krung Sri* — Krung Sri Rd. 50-70B. *New Hotel* — 22 Tanasarn Rd. 60-160B, some air-con rooms. *Amarin* — Tesaban 1 Rd. 70-130B, air-con.

Southern Thailand

Although under Thai political domination for several centuries, the South has always remained culturally apart from the other regions of Thailand. Historically the peninsula has been linked to cultures in ancient Indonesia, particularly the Srivijaya empire, which ruled a string of principalities in what is today Malaysia, southern Thailand, and Indonesia. The Srivijaya dynasty was based in Sumatra and lasted nearly five hundred years (8th-13th centuries). The influence of Malay-Indonesian culture is still apparent in the ethnicity, religion, art, and language of the *Thai pak tai*, the southern Thais.

The *Thai pak tai* dress differently, build their houses differently, and eat differently than their countrymen in the north. Many are followers of Islam, so there are quite a few mosques in southern cities; men often cover their heads and the long *sarong* is favored over the shorter *phaakama* worn in the northern, central and north-eastern regions. There are also a good many Chinese living in the South — the influence of whom can be seen in the old architecture and in the baggy Chinese pants worn by non-Muslims. All speak a dialect common among southern Thais that confounds even visitors from other Thai regions — diction is short and fast: *pai nai* (where are you going?) becomes *p'nai, tam arai* (what are you doing?) *tam'rai*, and the clipped tones fly into the outer regions of intelligibility, giving the aural impression of a tape played at the wrong speed.

Southern Thais are stereotypically regarded as rebellious folk, considering themselves reluctant subjects of Bangkok rule and Thai (central Thai) custom. Indeed, Thai Muslims (ethnically Malay) living in the provinces bordering on Malaysia complain of persecution by Thai government troops who police the area for insurgent activity. There has even been some talk of these provinces seceding from Thailand, an event that is highly unlikely to occur in the near future.

Bounded by water on two sides, the people of south Thailand are a sea-faring lot. One consequence of this natural affinity with the ocean is an abundance of delectable seafood, prepared southern-style. Brightly painted fishing boats, hanging nets, and neat thatched huts add to the *pak tai* setting; the traveller who does a stint in south Thailand is likely to come face to face with more than a few visions of 'tropical paradise', whatever his/her expectations might be. Three of Thailand's most important exports — rubber, tin, and coconut — are produced in the South so that the standard of living is a bit higher here than in other provincial regions.

HUA HIN

230 km south of Bangkok. A favourite beach resort for Thais, Hua Hin has a nice beach and a nifty old colonial-style Railway Hotel just off the beach. The Thais seem to want to keep this one for themselves, since it is seldom mentioned in any of the TAT literature. I don't blame them, Hua Hin is a

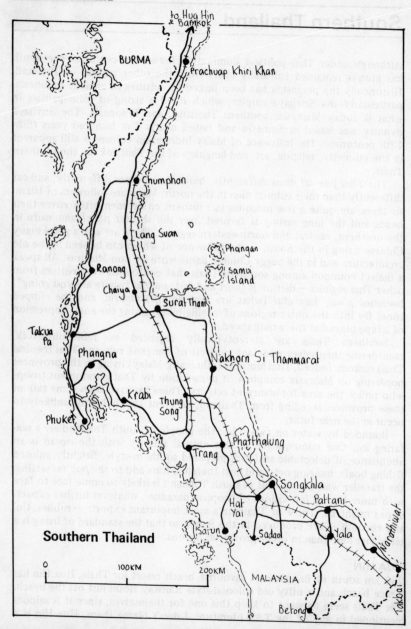

to Hua Hin & Bangkok

BURMA

Prachuap Khiri Khan

Chumphon

Lang Suan

Phangan

Ranong

Samui Island

Chaiya

Surat Thani

Takua Pa

Phangna

Nakhorn Si Thammarat

Krabi

Thung Song

Phuket

Phatthalung

Trang

Songkhla

Southern Thailand

Hat Yai

Pattani

Satun

Sadao

Yala

Narathiwat

0   100KM   200KM

MALAYSIA

Betong

Takbai

nice, quiet place to get away from it all and yet is a convenient distance from Bangkok.

Rama VII had a summer residence built here, right on the beach, which is still used by the royal family. Just north of the palace are Hua Hin's rickety piers, bustling with activity in the early morning when the fishing boats go out and in the evening when they return. A few of the piers are used exclusively for drying squid, thousands of them, and this part of town exudes a powerful aroma.

The main swimming beach, not Thailand's best, has thatched umbrellas and long chairs. Vendors from the nearby food stalls will bring loungers steamed crab, mussels, beer, etc, and there are pony rides for the kids.

Getting There (and heading south in general)

Air-con buses to Hua Hin are available from the Southern Bus Terminal on Charan Sanitwong Rd in Thonburi. The one-way fare is 74B and buses depart at 6.30 am, 7.20 am, 8.55 am, 10.20 am, 11.05 am, 12.55 pm, 2.05 pm, 3.25 pm, 4.55 pm, 6.20 pm, and 7.15 pm and make the trip in about four hours.

Several trains run between Bangkok and Hat Yai in the South, stopping in Hua Hin. The International Express, train No. 11 to Butterworth, leaves Sundays, Tuesdays, and Thursdays at 4.10 pm from Hualamphong Station, stopping in Hua Hin at 8.36 pm. Another Express (No. 11/15), terminating in Sungai Kolok on the Malaysian border, leaves on Mondays, Wednesdays, Fridays, and Saturdays at 4.10 pm also, arriving in Hua Hin at the same time as the Butterworth Express. Only first and second class cars are available on these Express trains; second class fare to Hua Hin is 79B. Three Rapid trains pass through Hua Hin daily: No. 43, leaving Bangkok at 12.10 pm, No. 41, leaving Bangkok at 7.50 pm, and No. 45, leaving at 6.25 pm; all arrive in Hua Hin approximately 4½ hours later. Basic fares for these trains are the same as for the Express — only the surcharge is different (25B for Express, 15B for the Rapid).

CHAIYA

About 640 km from Bangkok, just north of Surat. Best visited as a day trip from Surat Thani, Chaiya is one of the oldest cities in Thailand, dating back to the Srivijaya empire. In fact, the name may be a contraction of Siwichaiya, the Thai pronunciation, as Chaiya was a regional capital between the 8th and 10th centuries. Previous to this time the area was on the Indian trade route in South-East Asia. Many Srivijaya artifacts at the National Museum in Bangkok were found in Chaiya, including the Avalokitesvara Bodhisattva bronze, considered to be a masterpiece of Buddhist art. The restored *Borom That Chaiya* stupa at *Wat Phra Mahathat*, just outside of town, is a fine example of Srivijaya architecture, and strongly resembles the *chandis* of central Java. A ruined stupa at nearby *Wat Kaew*, also from the Srivijaya period, again shows central Javanese influence (or perhaps vice versa) as well as Cham (9th-century South Viet Nam) characteristics.

Another attraction for visitors to Chaiya is *Wat Suanmoke*, west of Wat Kaew, a modern forest *wat* founded by Buddhadasa Bhikkhu (Thai: *Phutthathat)*, Thailand's most famous monk. Buddhadasa, a rotund octogenarian, ordained as a monk when he was 21 years old, spent many years studying the Pali scriptures, and then retired to the forest for six years of solitary meditation. Returning to ecclesiastical society, he was made abbot of Wat Phra Mahathat, a high distinction, but conceived of Suanmoke ('garden of liberation') as an alternative to orthodox Thai temples. The philosophy that has guided Buddhadasa is ecumenical in nature, comprising Zen, Taoist, and Christian elements, as well as the traditional Theravada schemata. Today the hermitage is spread over 60 hectares of wooded hillside, and features huts for 40 monks, a museum-library, and a 'spiritual theatre'. This latter building has bas-reliefs on the outer walls which are facsimiles of sculpture at Sanchi, Bharhut and Amaravati in India. The interior walls feature modern Buddhist painting, eclectic to say the least, executed by the resident monks. An interesting and peaceful place.

Getting There
If you're going to Surat by train, you can get off at the small Chaiya railway station, then later grab the next train on to Surat. From Surat you can either hire a taxi or get a train going north from Surat's train station at Phun Phin. Taxis are best hired from Phun Phin, too. The trains between Surat and Chaiya may be full but you can always stand or squat in a third class car for the trip.

SURAT THANI/BAN DON
651 km from Bangkok. There is little of particular historical interest at Surat, a busy commercial centre and port dealing in rubber and coconut, but the town has character nonetheless. This is the first point in a south-bound journey towards Malaysia that really feels and looks like south Thailand. For most people Surat is only a stop on the way to Koh Samui, a luscious island 32 km off the coast, so that Ban Don, a Surat *amphoe* on the east, becomes the centre of attention.

The daily boats to Koh Samui leave from Ban Don, proceeding into the Gulf of Thailand from the River Tapi for the three-hour trip. Actually, Ban Don is a great place to wander about while waiting for a boat to Samui. There is a fabulous fruit market along the waterfront, and several good all-purpose 'general stores' and pharmacies on the street opposite the pier — good deals on *phaakamas* and Thai work shirts, as well as a place to pick up some mosquito repellent for Samui. Lots of good restaurants can be found in Surat/Ban Don, too (see 'Eating & Sleeping').

Getting There

Air-con buses leave the Southern Bus Terminal in Thonburi every evening at 8.30 pm, arriving in Surat 11 hours later; the fare is 150B. Several private tour companies also run buses to Surat from Bangkok, fares are usually 200+B.

Non air-con buses leave the same terminal at 8 am, 8 pm, and 10 pm for 50B less.

Trains for Surat, which don't really stop in Surat town but in Phun Phin, 14 km west of town, leave Hualamphong Station daily at 2.30 am, 12.10 pm, 4.10 pm, and 6.25 pm, arriving almost 12 hours later at their destination. There is also a Rapid train which leaves daily out of Thonburi's Bangkok Noi station at 2 am, arriving in Phun Phin at 2.30 pm. Basic fares are 191B for second class seats, 92B for third. Add 25B surcharge for Express, 15B for Rapid. Sleepers are available on the overnight trains.

Buses to Ban Don from Phun Phin railway station, for boats to Koh Samui, leave regularly throughout the day (about every 15 minutes) for 5B per passenger.

Note: It can be difficult to get a train out of Surat (Phun Phin) — it is better to book a bus out of Surat itself, especially if proceeding south. The trains are very often full, and it's a drag to take the bus to the station 14 km from town to be turned away. The railway will sell you 'standing room only' third class tickets to Bangkok or Hat Yai, however. For bus tickets try Southern Tours, at the Muang Thong Hotel in Surat, or Pak Tai Tour Office on Na Muang Rd. Siam Tours in Surat is not as good — both companies charge 130B one-way to Songkhla/Hat Yai.

KOH SAMUI

Samui Island long ago attained a somewhat legendary status among Asian travellers, yet it never really escalated to the touristic proportions of other similar getaways found between Goa and Bali. This is not to say that you'll be the only *farang* on the island if you go there — far from it. But Samui is still rather quiet and relatively unexploited. As long as water transportation is the only link to the mainland it will probably remain that way.

Samui is different than other islands in south Thailand and its inhabitants refer to themselves as *chao samui* — 'Samui folk' — rather than Thais. They are even friendlier than the average upcountry Thai, in my opinion, and have a great sense of humour. The island also has a distinctive cuisine, influenced by the omnipresent coconut fruit, the main source of income for *chao samui*. Coconut palms blanket the island, from the hillocks right up to the beaches, and two million coconuts are shipped to Bangkok each month. The durian, rambutan, and langsat fruits are also cultivated on Samui. The main island of the Samui group, Koh Samui, is Thailand's third largest, 247 square km, and is surrounded by 80 more smaller islands. Six of these, Pangan, Ta Loy, Tao, Tan, Ma Koh, and Ta Pao are inhabited as well.

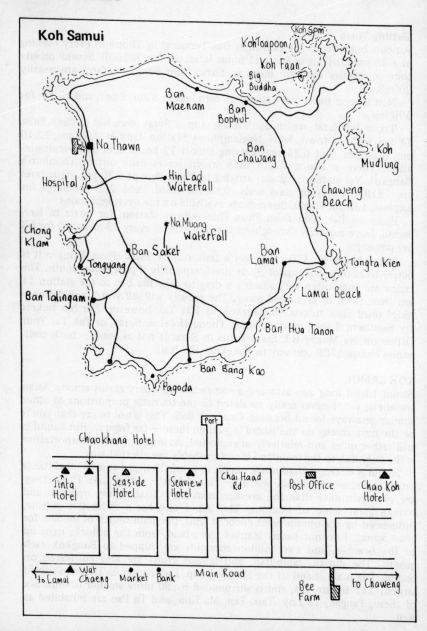

Koh Samui

Koh Spm
KohToapoon
Koh Saan
Big Buddha
Koh Samui
Ban Maenam
Ban Bophut
Ban Chawang
Koh Mudlung
Na Thawn
Hin Lad Waterfall
Hospital
Chaweng Beach
Na Muang Waterfall
Chong Klam
Ban Saket
Ban Lamai
Tongyang
Ban Talingam
Tongta Kien
Lamai Beach
Ban Hua Tanon
Ban Bang Kao
Pagoda

Port

Chaokhana Hotel

Tinta Hotel
Seaside Hotel
Seaview Hotel
Chai Haad Rd
Post Office
Chao Koh Hotel

to Lamai
Wat Chaeng
Market
Bank
Main Road
Bee Farm
to Chaweng

The population of Samui Island, approximately 32,000, is for the most part concentrated in the port town of Na Thawn, on the west side of the island facing the mainland, and in 10 or 11 small villages scattered around the island. One partially paved road encircles the island with several side roads poking into the interior; this main road is currently being upgraded so that it will eventually be paved all the way around.

Besides the beaches and rustic, thatched roof bungalows, Samui has a couple of waterfalls. *Hin Lad* waterfall is about 3 km from Na Thawn, and is a worthwhile visit if you're waiting in town for a boat back to the mainland. You can easily get there on foot — walk a 100 metres or so south of town on the main road, turning left at the road by the hospital. Go straight on this road to arrive at the falls. *Na Muang* waterfall, in the centre of the island 10 km from Na Thawn, is more scenic and less frequented. A *songthaew* from Na Thawn to these latter falls should be about 10B. *Songthaews* can also be hired at Chaweng and Lamai Beaches.

For temple enthusiasts there is at the southern end of the island, near the village of Bang Kao, *Wat Laem Saw* with an interesting old *chedi*. At the northern end, on a small rocky island joined to Samui by a causeway, is the so-called Temple of the Big Buddha. The modern image, about 12 metres in height, makes a nice silhouette against the tropical sky and sea behind it. The image is surrounded by *kutis*, or meditation huts, mostly unoccupied. The monks like receiving visitors there, though a sign in English requests that proper attire (no shorts) be worn on the temple premises.

As for beaches, there are several to choose from, but, as transportation around the island is rather irregular, plan to stay at the first one you get out at, at least until the next day when another truck comes around. The two main beaches at which most travellers rent bungalows are Chaweng and Lamai. The former has more bungalow 'villages', 11 at last count, with more under construction. Chaweng also is the longest beach, over twice the size of Lamai, and has the island of Mat Lang opposite. Both beaches have clear blue-green waters; Lamai is a little quieter, though neither place is particularly lively, and has a coral reef for snorkelling and underwater sightseeing.

If it's real peace and quiet you want, try Bophut, Big Buddha, or Thong Yang Beaches. The first two are part of a bay that holds Koh Faan (the island with the 'big Buddha'), separated by a small headland. The water here is not quite as clear as at Chaweng or Lamai but the feeling of seclusion is greater, so if you're the Robinson Crusoe type this may be it. Thong Yang Beach is located on the west side of the island, and is secluded (only one set of bungalows there), but the beach isn't that great by Samui standards. There is also Ang Thong Beach, just north of Na Thawn, very rocky but with more local colour (eg fishing boats) than the others.

Nearby *Koh Pangan*, an hour's boat ride north of Koh Samui, is worth a visit for its deserted beaches and coral formations, if you like snorkelling. In the interior of this somewhat smaller island is *Tran Sadet* waterfall.

Getting There

Two express boats go to Samui daily from Ban Don and each takes 2½-3 hours to reach the island. One leaves fairly regularly at 12.30 pm each day, but the other boat changes its departure schedule from time to time — last time I was there it was 9 am. Passage is now 50B. The upper deck is without seats but is more comfortable than the lower deck since you can stretch out. The most interesting people seem to choose the upper deck too -- Thai families who have brought picnic lunches to eat along the way, students on vacation, as well as *chao samui* gratefully returning from mainland business. Remember to take off your shoes for the highly polished upper deck.

There is also a slow boat for Samui that leaves the Ban Don pier each night at 11 pm, reaching Na Thawn around 5 am. This one costs 40B for the upper deck, 80B down below. Not recommended, unless you arrive in Surat too late for the fast boat and don't want to stay over in Ban Don.

The best time to visit the Samui group of islands is during the hot and dry season, February to late June. From July through October there is much rain to contend with, and between October and January heavy winds.

Boats to Koh Phangan leave Na Thawn, Koh Samui every day at 3.25 pm. The trip takes 45 minutes and costs 25B. Boats back to Samui leave Phangan's pier at 6 am daily.

NAKHORN SI THAMMARAT

814 km from Bangkok. Centuries before the eighth-century Srivijaya empire subjugated the peninsula, there was a city called Ligor or Lagor, capital of the Tambralinga kingdom, which was well-known throughout Oceania. Later, when Ceylon-ordained Buddhist monks established a cloister at the city, the name was changed to the Sanskrit *Nagara Sri Dhammaraja* ('City of the Sacred Dharma-King'), rendered in Thai phonetics as Nakhorn Si Thammarat. Thai shadow-play (*nang*) and classical dance-drama (*lakhorn*, Thai pronunciation of Lagor) are supposed to have been developed in Nakhorn Si Thammarat; buffalo-hide shadow puppets and dance masks are still made here.

Today Nakhorn Si Thammarat is known for its neilloware, a silver and black alloy/enamel jewellery technique borrowed from China many centuries ago. It is also, oddly enough, known for its 'gangsters'. Yes, the best hoodlums in Thailand supposedly come from NST, although I can't say I've ever met one.

Wat Mahathat is the city's most historic site, reputed to be over a thousand years old. Reconstructed in the mid-13th century, it features a 78-metre *chedi*, crowned by a solid gold spire weighing several 100 kilograms. The temple's *bot* contains one of Thailand's three identical Phra Singh Buddhas, one of which is supposed to have been originally cast in Ceylon before being brought to Sukhotahi (through Nakhorn Si Thammarat), Chieng Mai, and later, Ayuthaya. The other images are at Wat Phra Singh in Chieng Mai and the National Museum in Bangkok — each is claimed to be the original. Wat Mahathat is located at the south end of Ratchadamnoen Ave, the city's main street.

There are also three Hindu temples in NST, along Ratchadamnoen, inside the city walls. Brahmin priests from these temples take part each year in the royal ploughing ceremony in Bangkok. One temple holds a locally famous Shivalingam (phallic shrine) which is worshipped by women hoping to bear children.

Getting There

Air-con buses bound for Nakhorn Si Thammarat leave Bangkok's Southern Bus Terminal daily at 7.40 pm and 8.05 pm, arriving 12 hours later, fare 200B. Non air-con buses leave at 8 and 9 pm for about 50B less.

Southbound trains stop at the junction of Khao Chum Thong, about 30 km west of NST, from where you must take a bus or taxi to the coast. One train actually goes all the way to NST (there is a branch line from Khao Chum Thong to NST): the Rapid No. 47, which leaves Bangkok's Hualamphong station at 5.30 pm, arriving in NST at 9.35 am. Most travellers will not be booking a train directly to NST, but if you want to, second class fare is 238B, third class 113B.

From Surat Thani there are daily buses to Nakhorn. Check with the tour bus companies on Na Muang Rd. A tour bus from Surat to Nakhorn should run about 65B one-way. Buses run from Songkhla and Hat Yai to Nakhorn, too. Check with the Choke Dee Hotel in Songkhla or at one of the tour bus companies on Niphat-U-Thit 2 Rd in Hat Yai.

SONGKHLA

1320 km from Bangkok. Another former Srivijaya satellite on the east coast, not much is known about the pre-eighth century history of Songkhla, called Singora by the Malays. The city, small in area and population, is located on a peninsula between the *Thale Sap Songkhla* (an 'inland sea') and the South China Sea (or Gulf of Thailand, depending on how you look at it). The inhabitants are a colourful mixture of Thais, Chinese, and Muslims (ethnic Malays), and the local architecture and cuisine reflect the combination. The seafood served along the white Samila Beach is excellent, though the beach itself is not that great for swimming, especially if you've just come from Koh Samui. However, beaches are not Songkhla's main attraction, even if the TAT so promotes them — the town has plenty of other curiosities to offer. The evergreen trees along Samila Beach do give it a rather nice visual effect.

The waterfront on the inland sea is buzzing with activity most of the time. Ice is loaded onto fishing boats on their way out to sea, baskets and baskets of fish are unloaded onto the pier from boats just arrived, fish markets are setting up and disassembling, long boats doing taxi business between islands and mainland are tooling about. The fish smell along the piers is pretty powerful — be warned.

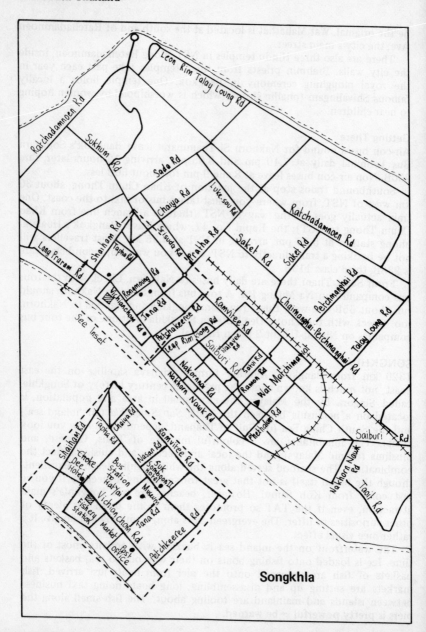

Songkhla

Leon Rim Talay Loung Rd
Ratchadamnoen Rd
Sukhum Rd
Sada Rd
Chaiya Rd
Luke sou Rd
Ratchadamnoen Rd
Shaiham Rd
Taphae Rd
Pratha Rd
Srisuda Rd
Saket Rd
Saket Rd
Lang Praram Rd
Ronmoung Rd
Petchmanghai Rd
Vichianchom Rd
Jana Rd
Ramvitee Rd
Chaimanghai-Petchmanghai Rd
Talay Loung Rd
See Inset
Petchakeeree Rd
Leap Rim Kong Rd
Naayvee Rd
Saiburi Rd
Satun Rd
Nakornna Rd
Ramon Rd
Wat Matchimat
Nakhon Nauk Rd
Phetthalon Rd
Saibuli Rd
Nakhon Nauk Rd
Taoit Rd

See Inset:
Shaiham Rd
Taphu Rd
Chaiya Rd
Ramvitee Rd
Choke Dee Hotel
Bus Station To Hatyai
Nasan Rd
Suk Sombon II Hotel
Sombon Hotel
Vichianchom Rd
Muuang Rd
Jana Rd
Fishery Station
Market
Petchkeeree Rd
Post Office

For interesting Songkhla architecture, walk along the back street parallel to the inland sea waterfront — Nakhorn Nawk Rd. Many of the buildings here are very old and show Chinese, Portuguese, and Malay influence. South of Samila Beach is a quaint Muslim fishing village — here is where the tourist photos of gaily painted fishing vessels are taken.

There is a *National Museum* in Songkhla, located in a 100-year old building of southern Thai-Chinese architecture, between Rongmoung Rd and Jana Rd (off Vichianchom Rd), next to Songkhla's bus station. Admission is free and there are exhibits from all national art style-periods, especially Srivijaya.

Wat Matchimawat, on Saiburi Rd towards Hat Yai, has an old marble Buddha image and a small museum. There is also an old *chedi* at the top of *Khao Noi*, a hill rising up at the north end of the peninsula.

Suan Tun, a topiary park located across from the Samila Hotel, has yew hedges trimmed into animal shape.

Koh Yaw (or Kaw Yaw), an island on the inland sea, is worth visiting just to see the cotton-weaving cottage industry there. The good-quality, distinctive *phaa kaw yaw* is hand-woven on rustic looms and available on the spot at 'wholesale' prices — meaning you still have to bargain but have a chance at undercutting the market price. Many different households around this thickly forested, sultry island are engaged in cotton-weaving, so it is best to go from place to place comparing prices and fabric quality. There are also a couple of *wats*, Khao Bo and Thai Yaw, to visit.

Boat taxis to Koh Yaw are available from the Songkhla inlet near the canal which feeds into the inland sea. The trip is 4B per person and boats are easiest to get in the morning around 7-8 am. An entire long boat to Koh Yaw, with pilot, can be rented for 70-100B, anytime of day.

Songkhla is south Thailand's educational centre; there is one university, several colleges, technical schools and research institutes, a nursing college, and a military training camp, all in or near the town.

Getting There

A Pak Tai Company tour bus from Surat to Songkhla/Hat Yai costs 130B one-way and leaves the Muang Thong Hotel in Surat at 4.45 am.

Air-con state-run buses leave Bangkok's Southern Bus Terminal daily at 6.30 pm, 7 pm, and 7.35 pm, arriving 19 hours later, for 220B. The privately-owned tour buses out of Bangkok (and there are several available) are quicker but cost around 260B.

For trains see Hat Yai below.

For getting around in town, *songthaews* circulate Songkhla and take passengers for 2B to any point on their route.

HAT YAI

1298 km from Bangkok. Hat Yai is south Thailand's commercial centre and one of the kingdom's largest cities, though it is only a district of Songkhla

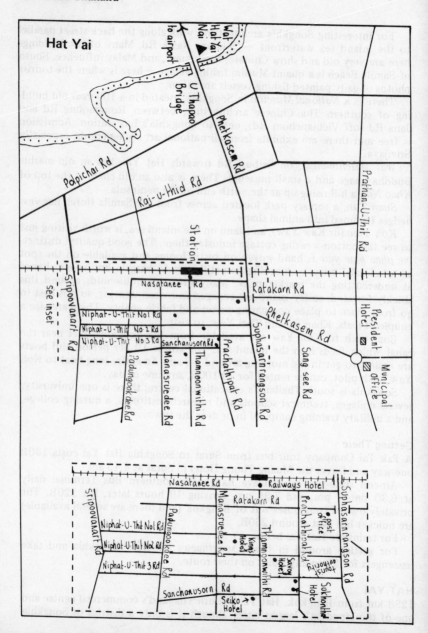

Hat Yai

province. A steady stream of customers from Malaysia keeps Hat Yai's downtown business district booming. Everything from dried fruit to stereos are sold in the shops along Niphat-U-Thit Rds Nos. 1, 2, and 3, not far from the railway station. *Songthaews* around Hat Yai cost 4B per person. Many travellers stay in Hat Yai, taking side trips to Songkhla, but I would recommend the opposite.

West of town a few km, off Phetkasem Rd towards the airport, is *Wat Hat Yai Nai*. A very large reclining Buddha on the premises (Phra Phut Mahatamongkon) is currently being restored along with the *wiharn* to house it. Inside the image's gigantic base is a curious little museum/souvenir shop/ mausoleum. The old abbot likes receiving visitors. To get there, hop on a *songthaew* near the intersection of Niphat-U-Thit 1 Rd and Phetkasem, get off after crossing the U Thapao Bridge.

Bullfighting, involving two bulls in opposition rather than man and bull, takes place as a spectator sport twice monthly in Hat Yai. On the first Sunday of each month it's at an arena next to the Nora Hotel off Thamnoonwithi Rd (the same road which leads to the railway station), and on the second Sunday it is at the Hat Yai Arena on Route 4, near the airport. Matches take place consecutively all day from 10.30 am until 6 pm and admission is only 5B — although many hundred times that amount exchanges hands during the non-stop betting by Thai spectators.

Getting There

From Songkhla big green buses leave every 15 minutes from Rongmoung Rd, across from the Songkhla National Museum, around the corner from the Songkhla Hotel, or they can be flagged down anywhere along Vichianchom Rd or Saiburi Rd, towards Hat Yai. The fare for these buses is 7B. Back to Songkhla from Hat Yai the green buses can be boarded anywhere along Niphat-U-Thit 2 Rd. For buses from Bangkok to Hat Yai, see the section on Songkhla, above.

Trains from Bangkok to Hat Yai leave Hualamphong daily at 2.30 pm (Express No. 19), 4.10 pm (Express 11/15), 12.10 pm (Rapid No. 43) and 6.25 pm (Rapid No. 45), arriving in Hat Yai at 7 am, 8.19 am, 10.28 am, and 2.28 pm. The basic fare is 267B second class or 126B third.

Thai Airways flies to Hat Yai daily at 5 pm, arriving at 6.15 pm. Tuesday, Thursday and Saturday there is also an 8 am flight, Monday there is a 10.45 am flight, and Friday an additional 1 pm flight. Flight time for all is about 75 minutes. Air fare is 1530B one-way.

PHUKET

885 km from Bangkok. The 'Pearl of the South', as the tourist industry has dubbed it, is Thailand's largest island (810 sq km) and a province in itself. Tin and tourism are Phuket's big moneymakers, yet the island is big enough to accommodate escapists of all budget levels. Formerly called Koh Thalang ('Phuket' and 'Thalang' are both Malay names), Phuket has a culture all its

KRABI

996 km from Bangkok, 180 km from Phuket town. A typical provincial southern town, Krabi has good beaches nearby, friendly townspeople, and good food. Accommodation here is cheap and boats can be chartered out to Koh Phi Phi, two islands where swallow nests are collected for 'bird's nest soup'. The beaches are deserted and prehistoric cave paintings can be seen.

Getting There

Catch buses to Krabi from Phuket's bus terminal on Phangnga Rd, same as for Phangnga. Fare should be about 50B. Buses to Krabi also leave out of Phangnga town.

PROCEEDING FURTHER SOUTH

By Train

Bangkok to Butterworth/Penang Sunday, Tuesday, and Thursday the International Express leaves Bangkok's Hualamphong Station at 4.10 pm, arriving in Hat Yai at 10.28 am the next day, and in Butterworth, Malaysia, at 5.46 pm (Malaysia time, 20 minutes ahead of Thailand). Fare to Butterworth is 359B second class, 183B third class, plus a 25B Express charge. Sleepers are available in second class only.

Bangkok to Kuala Lumpur Same train as above, changing to the Malayan Express in Butterworth and departing there for KL at 10.20 pm. Fare to KL is 528B second class, 288B third.

Bangkok to Singapore Same procedure as above, final leg leaves KL at 9 am, arriving in Singapore at 5.42 pm. The entire two-day journey costs 713B second class, 404B third.

Bangkok to Sungai Kolok If you prefer the east coast passage to Malaysia, there are Express trains to Sungai Kolok on Monday, Wednesday, Friday, and Saturday at 4.10 pm, arriving in SK at 2.55 pm. Second class fare is 323B, third is 152B, plus the Express charge, 25B.

By Yacht

The *Syzygie* sails from Phuket to Penang periodically between 1 December and 30 April. A two to three day trip costs US$80, six days for US$180. Contact the operators at Restaurant Number Four, Patong Beach, Phuket.

Encounter Overland's *Gypsy* does a similar trip for US$150-300, contact them at Patong Beach Bungalows.

By Air

Phuket to Penang Friday and Sunday Thai Airways departs Phuket at 12.50 pm, arriving in Penang at 2.10 pm (local time). One-way fare is 910B.

own, combining Chinese and Portuguese influences, like Songkhla, with that of the indigenous ocean-going peoples. Located in the Andaman Sea off south Thailand's west coast, the island's terrain is incredibly varied, with rocky beaches, long, broad, sandy beaches, limestone cliffs, forested hills, and tropical vegetation of all kinds. Great seafood is available all over the island and several off-shore islands are known for good snorkelling and scuba-diving.

Comparisons with Koh Samui, off the east coast, are inevitable as well as odious. All in all, there is more to do in Phuket, but that means more to spend your money on, too. There are more tourists in Phuket but they are concentrated at certain beaches — Patong and Rawai, for example. A beach like Nai Harn, which has only three bungalow groups so far, is just as quiet as Big Buddha Beach at Koh Samui. The feel of the islands is different — Samui is much further out in the sea and as such gives one more a feeling of adventure than Phuket, which is connected to the mainland by a bridge. Transport around Phuket is more regular than at Samui, and there are more motorcycles to rent. Ultimately it's a matter of personal preference; try both if you have the time.

The town of Phuket, located at the south-eastern end of the island, has some interesting markets — good place to buy baggy Chinese pants and *sarongs* — many decent restaurants, several cinemas, but little else of interest. Rather than stay in town it's best to rent a bungalow at one of the island's many beaches. Walk up *Khao Rang*, sometimes called Phuket Hill, south-west of town, for a nice view of city, jungle and sea. Twenty km north of town is the *Ton Sai Waterfall National Park*; take Thep Kasatri Rd to the district of Thalang, turn right at the intersection for Ton Sai falls, three km down the road.

Also in Thalang district, just north of the crossroads near Thalang village, is *Wat Phra Thong*, Phuket's 'Temple of the Gold Buddha'. The image is half buried — those who have tried to excavate it have met with unfortunate consequences.

The island of Koh Sire, four km east of Phuket town and separated from the bigger island by a canal, has a sea gypsy village and a hill-top reclining Buddha.

Beaches in Phuket

Patong Directly west of Phuket town, Patong is a large curved beach around *Ao Patong*, Patong Bay. A couple of expensive bungalows here attract well-heeled tourists. Nice beach, though.

Songthaews to Patong leave from Ranong Rd, near the day market and Fountain Circle, fare is 5B.

Karon A long, gently curving beach with small sand dunes and evergreen trees. Karon used to be quite a spot for budget travellers, but now there are seven sets of bungalows, two of which charge over 200B per person. Not

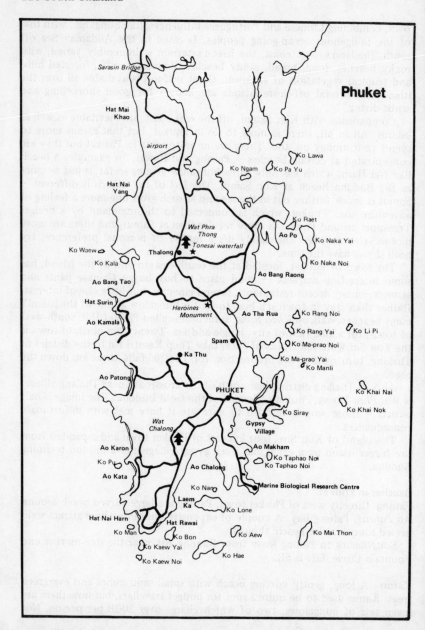

Sarasin Bridge

Hat Mai
Khao

airport

Ko Lawa

Hat Nai
Yang

Ko Ngam   Ko Pa Yu

Ko Raet

Wat Phra
Thong   Ao Po

Tonesai waterfall   Ko Naka Yai

Ko Waew   Thalong

Ko Kala   Ko Naka Noi

Ao Bang Raong

Ao Bang Tao

Hat Surin

Heroines
Monument   Ao Tha Rua   Ko Rang Noi

Ao Kamala

Ko Rang Yai   Ko Li Pi

Spam   Ko Ma-prao Noi

Ka Thu

Ko Ma-prao Yai
Ko Manli

Ao Patong

PHUKET   Ko Khai Nai

Ko Khai Nok

Wat Chalong   Ko Siray

Gypsy
Village

Ao Karon   Ao Makham

Ko Pu   Ko Taphao Noi
Ao Kata   Ko Taphao Noi

Ao Chalong

Ko Naro   Marine Biological Research Centre

Laem
Ka

Ko Lone

Hat Nai Harn

Ko Man   Hat Rawai

Ko Bon   Ko Aew   Ko Mai Thon

Ko Kaew Yai

Ko Kaew Noi   Ko Hae

Phuket

Getting There

From Hat Yai, non air-con buses leave the state bus station on Chevanusorn Rd, off Phetkasem, at 5.45 am, 7.45 am, 8.45 am, and 10 am daily, arriving in Phuket nine hours later for 78B. One air-con bus goes daily at 9.45 am from the same station, making the trip in seven hours for 120B.

From Bangkok, air-con buses leave the Southern Bus Terminal at 6.50 pm, 7.20 pm, and 7.50 pm. The trip takes 13-14 hours and the fare is 220B one-way, 374B round-trip. Several private tour buses run to Phuket regularly with fares from 220B to 280B. Most have one bus a day which leaves at 6 or 7 pm. The ride along the west coast between Ranong and Phuket can be hair-raising if you are awake, so it is fortunate that this part of the trip takes place during the wee hours of the morning.

Thai Airways has two flights a day to Phuket from Bangkok. There is one at 8 am each day, arriving at 9.10 am, except for Friday when it arrives at 9.55 due to a stopover in Surat. The second flight is at 11 am on Friday and Sunday, at 2.30 pm on Mondays, 4.50 pm on Wednesday and Saturday, and 1 pm Tuesday and Thursday. The fare is 1340B each way.

From Hat Yai there is a Thai Airways flight to Phuket daily at 1 pm, plus a 2.30 pm flight on Tuesday, Thursday, and Saturday. One-way fare is 410B. Tickets can be booked at th the Thai Airways office on Predaram Rd and Niphat-U-Thit 2 Rd in Hat Yai. The airport is 11 km west of town; inquire at the Thai Airways office or at one of the larger hotels for minibuses out to the airport.

PHANGNGA

94 km from Phuket town. The area around Phangnga Bay is quite scenic — lots of limestone cliffs, odd rock formations, islands that rise out of the sea like inverted mountains, not to mention caves and quaint fishing villages. Phangnga would make a good motorcycle trip from Phuket; bikes can be rented in Phuket town for 150-250B a day.

On the way to the town of Phangnga, turn left off Route 4 just five km past the small town of Takua Thung, to get to Tham Suwan Kuha, a cave temple full of Buddha images. Between Takua Thung and Phangnga town is the road to Tha Don, the Phangnga customs pier. It is at this pier that boats can be hired to tour Phangnga Bay, visiting a Muslim fishing village on stilts, half-submerged caves, strangely-shaped islands (yes, including those filmed in the 007 flick, *Man with the Golden Gun*), and other local oddities. Worthwhile if you have the bread.

Getting There

Buses for Phangnga leave from the Phuket bus terminal on Phangnga Rd, near the Thep Kasatri Rd intersection, hourly between 6.40 am and 3 pm. The trip to Phangnga town takes 1¾ hours and the one-way fare is 25B. Or rent a motorcycle.

much shade here, suntan guaranteed. See Kata (below) for transport to Karon.

Kata Just around a headland from Karon, Kata is more interesting as a beach, and is divided into two — Big Kata Bay and Little Kata Bay, *Ao Kata Yai* and *Ao Kata Noi*. The small island of Koh Pu is within swimming distance of the shore and on the way are some pretty nice coral reefs. The water here is very clear, and snorkelling gear can be rented from several of the bungalow groups. With seven sets of bungalows it almost gets crowded, but stays quiet just the same.

A few times daily a *songthaew* goes to both Kata and Karon from the Ranong Rd market in Phuket town, for 10B per person.

Nai Harn A few km south of Kata, on a small bay, this one is similar to Kata and Karon but less frequented — not much room for bungalow development here. Nai Harn is one of the cheapest beaches on Phuket. The TAT says Nai Harn beach is closed during the monsoon season (May to October) but I have been there in mid-September and it was quite open — the *songthaew* drivers in town will know one way or the other. Nai Harn is 18 km from town and a *songthaew* (leaving from the intersection of Bangkok Rd and Fountain Circle) costs 15B per person.

Rawai About 16 km from town (8B per person by *songthaew*, from Bangkok Rd) is Rawai, a fairly touristed beach with the big 88-room Rawai Resort Hotel. The beach is not so great but there is a lot happening in or near Rawai — a local sea gypsy village; Laem Ka beach (better than Rawai) to the north; boats to the nearby islands of Koh Lone, Koh Hae, Koh Hew, Koh Pi Pi, and others; and good snorkelling off Laem Phromthep at the southern tip of the island, easy to approach from Rawai. The diving around the offshore islands is great, especially at Kaew Yai/Kaew Noi, off Phromthep, and at Koh Hae. Shop around for boat trips to these islands for the least expensive passage — the larger the group, the cheaper the cost per person.

Surin North of Patong Bay, 24 km from Phuket town, Surin has a small beach and a fairly heavy surf. There is a golf course nearby. Just south of Surin Beach is Laem Singh (Cape Singh), a beautiful little rock-dominated beach. 10B by *songthaew* from Ranong Rd.

Nai Yang This one is near the Phuket airport, about 30 km from town. Nai Yang is a fairly secluded beach favoured by Thais, with only one set of bungalows; about five km further north along Route 402 (Thep Kasatri Rd) is Phuket's longest beach, Hat Mai Khao, where sea turtles lay their eggs between November and February each year.

EATING & SLEEPING IN SOUTH THAILAND

Hua Hin

The *Railway Hotel*, just off the beach on Damnoen Kasem Rd, is an old 'colonial-style' hotel (despite the fact that Thailand was never a colony) with big rooms, high ceilings, verandahs, and a restaurant with real tablecloths on the table — a great place to stay yet with very reasonable rates. Rooms with fan, bathroom, and verandah start at 90B. Air-con rooms can cost twice that, and there are 200B suites available. Cheaper rooms, 60B up, are available at the less charming *Chatchai* (59/1 Phetkasem Rd) in town and the *Damrong* (46 Phetkasem).

Great seafood is available at the night market in town, also on the beach. The Railway Hotel has *farang* food, in addition to Thai and local specialities.

Chaiya

Stay in Surat for visits to Chaiya or request permission to stay in the guest quarters at Wat Suanmoke.

Surat Thani

Several reasonable hotels are located along Na Muang Rd, not far from Ban Don.

Muang Thong — 428 Na Muang Rd. Clean, comfortable, doubles from 90B with fan; air-con rooms also available.

Pan Fah — 247 Na Muang Rd. 35B-80B; not particularly clean but adequate.

Surat — Near the Muang Thong on Chon Kasem Rd, off Na Muang. Quiet, adequate rooms for 70B.

Prem Suk — Na Muang Rd, across the street from the Muang Thong. Rooms from 35B.

Ban Don — Na Muang. Rooms from 50B.

The market near Surat's bus station has good cheap food. In Ban Don try the places along the waterfront road. The restaurant on the third floor of the Muang Thong Hotel has good breakfasts and *kow tom*.

Koh Samui

There are many places to stay on the beaches but they are all pretty similar in cost and amenities. It depends a lot on the acting proprietors of each bungalow as to how comfortable or hospitable a stay you'll have — Niyom, the proprietor of Big Buddha Bungalows, told me that all the bungalows along Chaweng, Big Buddha, and Lamai Beaches (about 19 groups in all) belong to only four different families. Niyom's family, for example, owns Big Buddha, Joy, Mellow, and Chaweng Bungalows.

At Big Buddha Beach, *Big Buddha Bungalow* is recommended. Niyom's sense of humour and *chai yen* (Thai for 'cool heart') make for a good atmosphere here. Double bungalows for 30B — bigger bungalows, really nice, go for 40-50B. Good view of the sunset; clean, quiet, bungalows, and excellent food add up to a memorable visit. There is another bungalow village nearby, *Peing Chai*, also with 30B rates.

At Bophut Beach, *Peace*, *Chaihaat*, and *Neet* have bungalows for 30B up. *Peace* is recommended.

Chaweng Beach had 11 bungalow villages strung along at the time of writing, with more under construction. They are all about the same and all start at 40B for a small bungalow. If there are a lot of vacant huts, you can sometimes talk the proprietors down to 30B, even less for lengthy stays if you put up a substantial deposit.

The food can vary a lot from 'village' to 'village' on Chaweng. Generally the restaurants at or near the *Chaweng Guest House Bungalows* are the best, though you do not have to stay there to eat there, of course. This part of Chaweng is where the night scene is, too, with amplified music, fish roasts, and impromptu beach parties. If you like quieter evenings, station yourself further north on the beach.

Bad reviews for *First* and *Sunshine* bungalows for inhospitable staff and lousy food. *Joy Bungalow* is comfortable and quiet, but the food's not that great there, either.

Recommended are *Sak*, *Tawee*, *Long Beach*, *Seaside*, and *Wisan*, but have a look around before you decide. There are miles of beach and bungalows at Chaweng.

At Lamai Beach rates are about the same as at Chaweng, sometimes more since a lot of snorkellers come here. Recommended for cleanliness and friendliness are *White Sand* or *Palm Beach*, but there are five others to choose from, all around 30-40B for a small bungalow.

Tong Yang has only one bungalow, the *Seagarden*, starting at 40B per hut.

Na Thawn (the port town), if you want or need to stay in Samui's largest habitation, has nine hotels to choose from, including the expensive (by Samui standards) *Chao Koh Hotel*, 80-120B doubles, and the cheaper *Seaside*, *Sri Samui*, *Chai Tale*, *Samui Bungalow*, *Chaokhana*, *Jinta*, *Seaview*, and *Roongraj*, all charging 30-50B per room.

Nakhorn Si Thammarat

In the 80-200B range there is the *Siam*, 1407/17 Chamramvithee Rd; *Neramit*, 1629 Neramit Rd; and the *Thai*, 1369 Ratchadamnoen Rd.

In the 50-120B range, choose from *Muang Thong*, 1459/7 Charoen Wattana Rd; *Nakhorn*, 1477/5 Yomaraj Rd; *Burapha*, Tambon Ta Wang; or *New Sri Thong*, both at Tambon Ta Wang; *Soonthon* or *Thiem Fa*, both at Tambon Si Chon.

Songkhla

Best deal in Songkhla is the *Songkhla Hotel*, on Vichianchom Rd across from the Fishing Station. The 80B rooms are very clean and comfortable; towels and purified water go with the room. Also good, but less quiet, is the *Choke Dee*, just down the road from the Songkhla. Similar rooms there are also 80B per double. The *Suk Somboon II* on Saiburi Rd, near the museum, is not bad for 70B a double.

There are lots of good restaurants in Songkhla but a few tend to over-charge foreign tourists. The Chinese restaurant on the corner opposite the Choke Dee Hotel is a rip-off, it looks good but walk on by unless you think 25B for fried rice is reasonable. The best seafood place, according to the locals, is the *Raan Ahaan Tae* on Tang Ngam Rd (off Songkhlaburi Rd and parallel to Saiburi Rd). The seafood on the beach is pretty good too — try the curried crab claws or spicy fried squid.

A great day and night market off Vichianchom Rd offers excellent market fare — a couple of stalls feature tasty Muslim food in addition to the usual Thai-Chinese selections. The local Muslim specialty is *khao mok kai*, a chicken biryani of sorts.

Hat Yai

Hat Yai has dozens of hotels within walking distance of the Railway Station. The *Railway Hotel* itself is pretty nice, though it costs a bit extra — 79B single, 99B double. In the same price range is the *King's Hotel*, on Niphat-U-Thit 3 Rd.

Cheaper rooms may be had at the *How Hua*, on the corner of Than-noonwithi and Niphat-U-Thit 3 Rd, four blocks from the railway station — 50B for a single, 80B double. Three-and-a-half blocks from the railway station is the *Savoy* on Niphat-U-Thit 2 Rd, with 80B doubles — nice place. Then five blocks from the station on Thannoonwithi Rd (corner of Sanchanusorn Rd) is another good find, the *Seiko*, with 60B singles, 80B doubles.

All of the above offer rooms with ceiling fans, no air-con. For air-con, check the *President* (near the Municipal Office on Prathan-U-Thit Rd) which has double rooms from 150B, and the *Sukhontha* (right around the corner from the TAT office, on Prachathipat Rd), with rooms from 200B. The Sukhontha also has a bowling alley, a massage parlour, and a night club.

Lots of good, cheap restaurants can be found along the three Niphat-U-Thit Rds, in the markets off side streets between them, and near the railway station. *Muslim-O-Cha*, a Muslim restaurant (no pork) across from the King's Hotel, has a good reputation and is usually crowded with Malaysian customers.

Four of Hat Yai's six cinemas have sound rooms where the original English soundtrack of English-language films can be heard while watching films that have dubbed-in Thai for the rest of the theatre; *Siam* (Phetkasem Rd), *Coliseum* (Pratchathipat Rd), *Chalerm Thai* (Suppasamongsan Rd) and the *Haadyai Rama* (Phetkasem Rd).

Phuket

In Town The *Rasda Hotel* opposite Phuket Teacher's College (Withayalai

Khru Phuket) on Thep Kasatri Rd has rooms from 80B, some with air-con, but it is a bit out of town. At 89 Phangnga Rd in the centre of town is the *Sin Tawee* with rooms from 70B. Also near the centre of town is the *Laem Thong*, one of Phuket's cheapest, at 13 Soi Rommani off Thalang Rd — all rooms are 50B, with fan. The *Charoensuk*, 136 Thalang Rd, has singles for 40B, doubles for 50B, with fan. Similar low rates can be found at the *On On* (19 Phangnga Rd) and the *Koh Sawan* (19/8 Poonpol Rd) — the latter is out towards the waterfront, the former near the market and *songthaew* terminal for most outlying beaches.

Rawai Beach *Pornmae Bungalow*, 58/1 Wiset Rd, all bungalows 50B.
P Hut — 27/2 Wiset Rd, Hat Mitthaphap Rd, 80B up.

Patong Beach The cheapest bungalows are the *Sea Dragon*, 80B and the *Patong Tropica*, which has bungalows for 80-250B. Several other hotels and bungalows — *Patong Inn*, *Royal Palm*, *Patong Seaside*, *Patong Bayshore*, *Pornkratheep* — are in the 150-200B range.

Nai Harn Three of the bungalow operations here are around 40B per night: *Bungalow Nai Harn*, *Pin*, and, farther north towards Kata Beach, *Ao Sane Beach*. A fourth, *Johnnie's*, reportedly has bungalows for only 15B. Food is good and reasonably priced at the beach restaurants here, including the special 'seasonal' mushroom omelette, made with *het khii khwai* — 'water-buffalo shit mushrooms'.

Kata Bungalow rates have really gone up at Kata in recent years; only four years ago there was only one bungalow village, with bungalows for 10B. Now there are seven, ranging from 40B at the *West Wind* to 300B at the *Ka Ka Ta*. The rest, *Taeo Ngam*, *Kata Shangri-La*, *Kata Villa*, *Kata Guest House*, and *Kata Tropicana*, are in the 50-80B range.

Karon Similar scene to Kata: seven bungalow groups, ranging from 40B to 260B. The *Dream Hut* and *My Friend* both go for 40-50B; the *Karon* for 60B; *Karon-on-Sea*, *Phuket Ocean Resort*, *Relax Bay Inn*, and the *Golden Sand* are all 200B and over. Good food is available but is slightly more expensive — food and accommodation rates go hand-in-hand at all the Phuket beaches.

Phang-nga

There are several hotels here in the 40-80B range: *Ratana Pong*, *Lak Muang*, and *Rak Phang-nga*, all on Phetkasem Rd, the main street of town, plus *Padoong*, *Takua Pa*, and *Tan Prasert*, all on the west end of town.

The *Phangnga Bay Resort* near the customs pier is beyond the means of most budget travellers (500-1000B) but has a swimming pool and a decent restaurant.

Krabi

Cheapest places to stay in town are the *New Hotel* (Uttarakit Rd) and the *Kittisook* (Phangnga Rd), both of which have 50-80B rooms. Slightly higher-priced but nicer, are the *Thai* (3 Adisom Rd) and the *Krabi* (Uttarakit Rd), at 80-100B.

The best hotel in town is the *Viengthong* at 155 Uttarakit Rd. The Coffee Shop has an English-language menu; rooms start at 100B.

The Penal Code of Thailand Against Sacrilege

OFFENCES RELATED TO RELIGION

Section 206: — Whoever commits any act, by any means whatever, to an object or a place of religious worship of any community in a manner likely to insult the religion shall be punished with imprisonment not exceeding three years or fine not exceeding six thousand baht, or both.

Section 207: — Whoever cause any disturbance at an assembly lawfully engaged in the performance of religious ceremonies shall be punished with imprisonment not exceeding one year or fine not exceeding two thousand baht, or both.

Section 208: — Whoever dresses or uses a symbol showing that he is a Buddhist priest or novice, holy/man or chergyman of any religion unlawfully in order to make another person believe that he is such person shall be punished with imprisonment not exceeding one year or fine not exceeding two thousand baht, or both.

Glossary

achaan — respectful title for teacher, from Sanskrit *acharya*.

ao — bay or gulf.

amphoe — district; next subdivision down from province. Sometimes spelled *amphur*

bhikku — Buddhist monk or priest.

bot — central sanctuary or chapel in a Thai temple.

chaihat — beach.

chedi — stupa; monument erected to house a Buddha relic; called *pagoda* in Burma, *dagoba* in Sri Lanka, *cetiya* in India.

doi — peak, as in mountain.

farang — foreigner of European descent.

hat — beach; short for *chaihat*.

isaan — general term for north-east Thailand, from the Sanskrit name for the mediaeval kingdom *Isana*, which encompassed parts of Cambodia and north-east Thailand.

jangwat — province.

Jataka — life-stories of the Buddha.

keo — also spelled *kaew*; crystal, jewel, glass, or gem.

koh — island.

laem — cape (in the geographical sense).

mae nam — river; literally 'mother water'.

Maha That — literally 'great element', from the Sanskrit-Pali *mahadhatu*; common name for temples which contain Buddha relics.

mondop — small square building in a *wat* complex generally used by lay people as opposed to monks; from the Sanskrit *mandapa*.

muang — city

nakhorn — city; from Sanskrit-Pali *nagara*

nam — water

nam phrik — pepper sauce.

nam plaa — fish sauce.

phaakma — piece of cotton cloth worn as a wraparound by men.

phaasin — same as above for women.

phra — monk or Buddha image; an honorific term from the Pali *vara*, excellent.

prang — Khmer style tower on temples.

prasat — small ornate building with a cruciform ground plan and needle-like spire, used for religious/royal purposes, located on *wat* grounds. From the Sanskrit term *prasada*.

samlor — literally 'three wheels'; three-wheeled pedicab used prominently in provincial Thailand.

sema — boundary stones used to consecrate ground used for monastic ordinations; from the Sanskrit-Pali *sima*.

soon — centre; from the Pali *sunya*.

songthaew — literally 'two rows'; common name for small pick-up trucks with two benches in the back, used as buses/taxis.

thale sap — inland sea.

tambon — also spelled *tambol*; next subdivision below *amphoe*; 'subdistrict' or 'precinct'.

thep — angel or divine being; from Sanskrit *deva*.

tuk-tuk — motorized *samlor*.

wat — temple-monastery; from Pali *avasa*, monk's dwelling.

wiharn — counterpart to *bot* in Thai temple, containing Buddha images but not circumscribed by *sema* stones; from Sanskrit *vihara*.

Index

Thai names

Listed below are the Thai names for a number of places and for various items of food and drink. The phonetic symbols in the romanization follow the method described on pages 20-21. Even if your pronunciation is not too good, you may be able to point to the Thai word, or else you can use the list to help recognise Thai names when you see them on signs or menus.

เครื่อง ดื่ม		**Beverages**
น้ำเปล่า	nam. plao.	plain water
น้ำต้ม	nam' tom!	boiled water
น้ำแข็ง	nam' khaeng?	ice
น้ำชา	nam' chaa	weak Chinese tea
น้ำร้อน	nam' rawn'	hot water
น้ำเย็น	nam' yen	cold water
ชาจีน	chaa jiin	Chinese tea
ชาเย็น	chaa yen	iced tea with milk & sugar
ชาดำเย็น	chaa dam yen	iced black tea with sugar (Thai tea)
ไม่ใส่น้ำตาล	mai! sai. nam'-taan	no sugar (command)
ชาดำร้อน	chaa dam rawn'	hot Thai tea with sugar
ชาร้อน	chaa rawn'	hot Thai tea with milk & sugar
กาแฟร้อน	kaafae rawn'	hot coffee with milk & sugar
โอเลี้ยง	oh-lieng'	iced coffee with sugar, no milk
โอวัลติน	ohwantin	Ovaltine
น้ำส้ม	nam' som!	orange soda
นมจืด	nom jeud.	plain milk
นมเปรี้ยว	nom priaw!	yoghurt
เบียร์	bia	beer
น้ำมะนาว	nam' manao	iced lime juice with sugar (usually with salt too)
ไม่ใส่เกลือ	mai! sai. kleua	no salt (command)
แม่โขง	mae khong?	rice whiskey

แกง		**Curries**
แกงมัสหมั่น	kaeng mat'-sa-man	rich, spicy curry with chicken or beef
แกงกะหรี่ไก่	kaeng kari. kai.	mild, 'Indian-style' curry with chicken
แกงเผ็ดไก่	kaeng phet. kai.	hot Thai chicken curry
แกงส้ม	kaeng som!	fish & vegetable curry
แกงเขียวหวาน	kaeng khiaw?waan?	'green' curry, made with fish, chicken or beef
แกงพะแนง	kaeng phanaeng	savoury curry with chicken or beef

127

| แกงเนื้อ | kaeng neua' | beef curry |
| แกงปลาดุก | kaeng plaa duk. | catfish curry |

ซูพ — Soups

แกงจืด	kaeng jeud.	mild soup with vegetables and pork
แกงจืดเต้าหู้	kaeng jeud. tao!hu!	same as above, with bean curd
ต้มข่าไก่	tom! khaa. kai.	delicious soup with chicken, 'laos', & coconut
ต้มยำกุ้ง	tom! yam kung!	shrimp & lemon grass soup with mushrooms
แกงจืดลูกชิ้น	kaeng jeud. luuk! chin'	fishball soup
ข้าวต้มปลา/ไก่/กุ้ง	khao! tom! plaa/ kai./kung!	rice soup with fish/chicken/shrimp

ไข่ — Eggs

ไข่ต้ม	khai. tom!	hard-boiled egg
ไข่ดาว	khai. dao	fried egg
ไข่เจียว	khai. jiaw	scrambled egg or plain omelette
ไข่ยัดไส้	khai. yat' sai!	omelette stuffed with vegetables and pork

กับข้าว — Rice Dishes

ข้าวผัดหมู/ไก่/กุ้ง	khao! phat. muu?/ kai./kung!	fried rice with pork/chicken/shrimp
ข้าวมันไก่	khao! man kai.	boned, sliced chicken with marinated rice
ข้าวหน้าไก่	khao! naa! kai.	chicken with sauce over rice
ข้าวหน้าเป็ด	khao! naa! pet.	roast duck over rice
ข้าวหมูแดง	khao! muu? daeng	'red' pork with rice

เส้นก๋วยเตี๋ยว/บะหมี่ — Noodles

ก๋วยเตี๋ยวน้ำ	kuaytiaw? nam'	wide rice noodle soup with vegetables & meat
ก๋วยเตี๋ยวแห้ง	kuaythiaw? haeng!	same as above without broth
ก๋วยเตี๋ยวแห้ง ราดหน้า	raat! naa!	same noodles served on plate with gravy
ก๋วยเตี๋ยวแห้ง ผัดไทย	phat. thai	thin rice noodles fried with vegetables, egg, peanuts
ก๋วยเตี๋ยวแห้ง ผัดซีอิ๊ว	phat. siyu'	fried thin noodles with soy sauce
บะหมี่น้ำ	bamii. nam'	wheat noodles in broth, with vegetables & meat
บะหมี่แห้ง	bamii. haeng!	same as above without broth

อาหารทะเล		**Seafood**
ปลาเปรี้ยวหวาน	plaa priaw!waan?	sweet & sour fish
ปูนึ่ง	puu neung!	steamed crab
ก้ามนึ่ง	kaam! chalaam?	steamed crab claws
หูฉลาม	huu? chalaam?	shark fin soup
ปลาทอด	plaa tawt!	crisp-fried fish
กุ้งทอด	kung! tawt!	fried prawns
กุ้งชุบแป้งทอด	kung! chup'baeng! tawt!	batter-fried prawns
ปลานึ่ง	plaa neung!	steamed fish
ปลาเผา	plaa phao?	grilled fish
วุ้นเส้นอบปู	wun' sen! op. puu	cellophane noodles baked with crab

		Miscellaneous
ผัดผักหลายอย่าง	phat. phak. lai? yang.	stir-fried vegetables
ผักบุ้งผัด	phak. bung! phat.	morning-glory vine fried in garlic & bean sauce
ปอเปี๊ยะ	paw-pia'	spring rolls
เนื้อผัดน้ำมันหอย	neua' phat. nam'man hawy?	beef in oyster sauce
เป็ดตุ๋น	pet. tun?	duck soup
เป็ดย่าง	pet. yang!	roast duck
ไก่ผัดใบกะเพรา	kai. phat. bai ka-phrao	chicken fried in holy basil
ไก่ย่าง	kai. yang!	roast chicken
ไก่ผัดพริก	kai. phat. phrik!	chicken fried with chiles
ไก่ทอด	kai. tawt!	fried chicken
สะเต๊ะ	sate'	'satay' or skewers of barbequed meat, sold on street
ส้มตำ	som! tam	spicy green papaya salad, speciality of the north-east
น้ำยา	nam' yaa	noodles with fish curry
พระรามลงสรงไก่	phra' raam longsong? kai.	chicken with vegetable & peanut sauce
ไก่ผัดเม็ดมะม่วง	kai. phat. met'mamuang!	chicken fried with cashews
กุ้งผัดพริกเผา	kung! phat. phrik' phao?	prawns fried with chilis
ไก่ผัดขิง	kai. phat khing?	chicken fried with ginger
เกี๊ยวกรอบ	kiaw' krawp.	fried wonton
ยำวุ้นเส้น	yam wun' sen!	cellophane noodle salad

ลาบเนื้อ	laap! neua'	spicy beef salad
ยำเนื้อ	yam neua'	hot & sour grilled beef salad
ไก่สับถั่วงอก	kai. sap. tua. ngawk!	chicken with bean sprouts
ทอดมันปลา	tɔwt! man plaa	fried fish cakes with cucumber sauce

ขนม		**Sweets**
สังขยา	sang?kha-yaa?	Thai custard
สังขยามะพร้าว	sang?kha-yaa?maphrao'	coconut custard
ฝอยทอง	fawy? thawng	sweet shredded egg yolk
หม้อแกง	maw! kaeng	egg custard
กล้วยบวดชี	kluay! buat. chii	banana in coconut milk
กล้วยแขก	kluay! khaek.	'Indian-style' banana, fried
ลูกตาลเชื่อม	luuk! taan cheuam!	sweet palm kernels
ตะโก้	takoh!	Thai 'Jello' with coconut cream
ข้าวเหนียวแดง	khao! niaw? daeng	sticky rice with coconut cream
ข้าวเหนียวมะม่วง	khao! niaw? mamuang!	sticky rice in coconut cream and ripe mango

ผลไม้		**Fruit**
แตงโม	taeng moh	watermelon
มังคุด	mang-khut'	mangosteen
เงาะ	ngaw'	rambutan
ชมพู่	chom phuu!	rose-apple
กล้วย	kluay!	banana; there are over 20 varieties — *kluay!-hawm?* is the best all-round
สับปะรด	sap.pa.rot'	pineapple
ละมุด	lamut'	'sapota'; eating too much of this plum-like fruit can irritate the stomach
มะไฟ	mafai	'rambeh', sweet, apricot-like.
มะม่วง	ma-muang!	mango, several varieties & seasons
ทุเรียน	turian	durian. Held in high esteem by the Thais, but most westerners dislike this fruit. There are several varieties, so keep trying.
ส้มโอ	som! oh	pomelo
ลำไย	lam yai	longan
มะละกอ	ma'la'kaw	papaya
น้อยหน่า	nawy' naa!	custard-apple

Place Names

Thai	Romanized	Thai	Romanized
พัทยา	Pattaya	นครสวรรค์	Nakhorn Sawan
เกาะสีชัง	Koh Si Chang	นครศรีธรรมราช	Nakhorn Si Thammarat
เกาะสมุย	Koh Samui	น่าน	Nan
กรุงเทพ ฯ	Bangkok (Krung Thep)	พังงา	Phang Nga
ศรีอยุธยา	Ayuthaya	พิษณุโลก	Phitsanuloke
เชียงใหม่	Chieng Mai	ภูเก็ต	Phuket
เชียงราย	Chieng Rai	ราชบุรี	Rajburi (Ratburi)
ชลบุรี	Chonburi	ร้อยเอ็ด	Roi Et
เชียงแสน	Chieng Saen	สระบุรี	Saraburi
ฝาง	Fang	สงขลา	Songkhla
กำแพงเพชร	Kamphaeng Phet	สบรวก	Sop Ruak
กาญจนบุรี	Kanchanaburi	สุโขทัย	Sukhothai
ขอนแก่น	Khon Kaen	สวรรคโลก	Sawankhaloke
กระบี่	Krabi	สุราษฎร์ธานี	Surat Thani
หัวหิน	Hua Hin	สุรินทร์	Surin
ลำพูน	Lamphun	ศรีราชา	Si Racha
ลพบุรี	Lopburi	อุบลราชธานี	Ubol Ratchathani
มหาสารคาม	Mahasarakham	อุดรธานี	Udorn Thani
นครพนม	Nakhorn Phanom	หาดใหญ่	Hat Yai
นครปฐม	Nakhorn Pathom	ไชยา	Chaiya
นครราชสีมา	Nakhorn Ratchasima (Khorat)		

LONELY PLANET NEWSLETTER

We collect an enormous amount of information here at Lonely Planet. Apart from our research we also get a steady stream of letters from people out on the road — some of them are just one line on a postcard, others go on for pages. Plus we always have an ear to the ground for the latest on cheap airfares, new visa regulations, borders opening and closing. A lot of this information goes into our new editions or 'update supplements' in reprints. But we'd like to make better use of this information so we are now producing a quarterly newsletter packed full of the latest news from out on the road. It appears in February, May, August and November of each year. If you'd like an airmailed copy of the most recent newsletter just send us A$1.50 (A$1 within Australia) or A$5 (A$4 in Australia) for a year's subscription.